An Archon Book on Popular Entertainments

A. H. SAXON, GENERAL EDITOR

The Autobiography of Mrs. Tom Thumb

"I will a plain unvarnished tale unfold."

THE AUTOBIOGRAPHY

of

Mrs. Tom Thumb

(Some of My Life Experiences)

by *COUNTESS M. LAVINIA MAGRI*

formerly Mrs. General Tom Thumb

with the assistance of Sylvester Bleeker

EDITED AND INTRODUCED BY

A. H. SAXON

1979

ARCHON BOOKS

HAMDEN   CONNECTICUT

Library of Congress Cataloging in Publication Data

Thumb, Tom, Mrs., 1841–1919.
The autobiography of Mrs. Tom Thumb

(An Archon book on popular entertainments)
Bibliography: p.
Includes index.
1. Thumb, Tom, Mrs., 1841–1919.
2. Circus performers—United States—Biography.
I. Bleeker, Sylvester, joint author.
II. Saxon, A. H.
III. Series.
GV1811.T55A33   791.3′092′4   [B]   78–26267
ISBN 0–208–01760–7

© A. H. Saxon 1979

First published 1979 as an Archon Book,
an imprint of The Shoe String Press, Inc.

Hamden, Connecticut 06514

Printed in the United States of America

Contents

List of Illustrations
page 6

Introduction
page 9

The Autobiography of Mrs. Tom Thumb
page 23

APPENDIX: Published Portions of the Autobiography
and Additional Recollections
page 175

Notes
page 180

Selected Bibliography
page 191

Index of Persons
page 195

5

Illustrations

MRS. GENERAL TOM THUMB. *Historical Collections, Bridgeport Public Library.* *frontispiece*

THE TITLE PAGE TO THE COUNTESS M. LAVINIA MAGRI'S AUTOBIOGRAPHY. *Courtesy of the New-York Historical Society, New York City.* *page 25*

A LEAF OF LAVINIA'S AUTOBIOGRAPHY. *Courtesy of the New-York Historical Society, New York City.* *page 122*

following page 32

LAVINIA AS A YOUNG GIRL. *Historical Collections, Bridgeport Public Library.*

LAVINIA AS A YOUNG WOMAN. *Historical Collections, Bridgeport Public Library.*

P. T. BARNUM ADMIRING ONE OF HIS "CURIOSITIES." Published by Mathew B. Brady. *Historical Collections, Bridgeport Public Library.*

"THE FAIRY WEDDING GROUP." Small *carte de visite* published by Mathew B. Brady, 1863. *Historical Collections, Bridgeport Public Library.*

"GEN. TOM THUMB, WIFE & CHILD." Published by Mathew B. Brady. *Historical Collections, Bridgeport Public Library.*

MINNIE WARREN AND COMMODORE NUTT IN HIS UNIFORM. Small *carte de visite. Historical Collections, Bridgeport Public Library.*

"THE LILLIPUTIAN CARD PARTY." Small *carte de visite* published by Mathew B. Brady, 1863. *Historical Collections, Bridgeport Public Library.*

TOM THUMB, LAVINIA, MINNIE WARREN, AND THEIR MANAGER SYLVESTER BLEEKER. *Historical Collections, Bridgeport Public Library.*

following page 128

A PORTLY TOM THUMB AND LAVINIA POSE ON A THEATRICAL BALCONY. Published by A. Bogardus of New York. *Historical Collections, Bridgeport Public Library.*

TOM THUMB IN HIS KNIGHTS TEMPLAR UNIFORM. Published by
George T. Putnam of Middleboro. *Historical Collections,
Bridgeport Public Library.*

LAVINIA IN HER WIDOW'S WEEDS. Published by Rocher and Beebe of
Chicago. *Historical Collections, Bridgeport Public Library.*

BARON ERNESTO MAGRI, LAVINIA, AND HER SECOND HUSBAND
COUNT PRIMO MAGRI. Published by Swords Bros. of York,
Pennsylvania. *Historical Collections, Bridgeport Public Library.*

LAVINIA IN WHITE. *Barnum Museum.*

COUNT PRIMO AND BARON ERNESTO MAGRI IN ONE OF THEIR BUR-
LESQUE SKITS. *Postcard in the Barnum Museum.*

DETAIL OF A PHOTOGRAPH OF LAVINIA AND COUNT MAGRI TAKEN IN
1914. *Barnum Museum.*

THE GRAVES OF TOM THUMB AND LAVINIA AND THE STRATTON FAMILY
MONUMENT IN BRIDGEPORT'S MOUNTAIN GROVE CEMETERY.
Photographed in the spring of 1978.

Introduction

THE AUTHOR OF THESE MEMOIRS, the Countess M. Lavinia Magri—who began life under the more plebeian name Mercy Lavinia Warren Bump, but eventually was known throughout the world as "Mrs. General Tom Thumb"—was born in the small Massachusetts town of Middleboro on 31 October 1841. Whether the date had anything to do with it, by the age of ten, as she informs us, she had attained no greater height and weight than twenty-four inches and twenty pounds, although she later added somewhat to these figures and at the time of her wedding to Tom Thumb in 1863 was reported to measure thirty-two inches and weigh as much as twenty-nine pounds.[1] She was, in fact, what people in her day and medical authorities in our own refer to as a "dwarf," but what those with more tender sensibilities—since she was perfectly proportioned and an example of what is known as ateliotic dwarfism, rather than of the more common disproportionate or achondroplastic variety—would today term a "midget." Her parents, both of normal size, were James S. and Huldah P. Bump, who produced a numerous family of sons and daughters. One other child, Huldah Pierce, was also a midget and was born on 2 June 1849.

After completing her education in the Middleboro school and briefly teaching there herself, Lavinia was literally launched on a career in show business by a cousin who managed a floating museum

9

of "curiosities" on the western rivers. Her experiences while touring by water are described in her autobiography, as is her "discovery" in 1862 by the enterprising showman P. T. Barnum, who astutely billed her under the shortened name Lavinia Warren and also induced her sister, renamed Minnie Warren, to enter his employ. Her highly publicized wedding to Tom Thumb followed almost immediately, and from then until her death in 1919 she was without question the world's most famous female midget, touring unremittingly in America and Europe and even, shortly after the West had been opened by the Union Pacific Railroad in 1869, embarking on a three-year tour around the world with the General Tom Thumb Company.

Although dwarfs had been publicly exhibited for centuries prior to Lavinia's arrival on the scene, it was Barnum, with his usual flair for publicity and showmanship, who raised such entertainments to an art form. His discovery in 1842 and subsequent exploitation of the Bridgeport "man in miniature" Charles Sherwood Stratton (1838–83), better known as General Tom Thumb, provided him with plenty of experience. These entertainments, it should be noted, were not of the "freak-show" type which one could see on the midways of most carnivals and circuses until a few years ago. Rather, they were fully developed, independent entertainments ("levees" is the word Lavinia herself uses in referring to them), consisting of songs, dances, impersonations, and dramatic skits. With the occasional addition of a "prestidigitateur," ventriloquist, or trained bird act, they easily made up a full evening's program. Tom Thumb himself, following his initial tutoring by Barnum, for years appeared in an entertainment of his own in which he impersonated such characters as an Oxonian, a Scottish Highlander, and Napoleon; danced the polka, sailor's hornpipe, and highland fling; sang such popular songs as "Come Sit Thee Down," "Dandy Jim," "Villikens and His Dinah," and "Then You'll Remember Me"; and performed, while wearing a body stocking simulating nudity, a series of "Grecian Statues" or tableaux vivants—the whole tied together by comic banter with a "Doctor" or straight man, who questioned the General about his personal history and his well-known partiality for the ladies (by the age of nineteen he was boasting he had kissed "about two millions and a half" of them) and invited children to come up on the stage so their heights could be compared with Tom Thumb's. While in Paris with Barnum in 1845, he had appeared at the Théâtre du Vaudeville in a play by Clairville and Dumanoir entitled *Le Petit Poucet*—in the course of whose action he was served up in a pie, ran between the legs of ballet dancers, and drove about the stage in a miniature carriage drawn by four ponies—and this work, adapted by Albert Smith as *Hop O' My Thumb*, was also in his repertoire. There was always some tiny furniture such as a settee on the stage, and during the daytime the act would be further advertised by the General's driving about in one of his miniature carriages (a famous blue one was presented to him by Queen Victoria), always tying up traffic, of course, and a frequent source of complaint before magistrates.

Lavinia's own early "levees" were not so extensive as Tom Thumb's, although she does mention the fatigue they entailed while she was traveling with Colonel Wood on his floating museum. In the main they consisted of songs such as "The Cottage by the Sea," "Annie of the Vale," and a chauvinistic piece entitled "E Pluribus Unum," and a good deal of time seems to have been spent in "conversing" with her visitors. In her memoirs she is obviously eager to avoid giving any impression of vulgar showmanship. Indeed, so genteel do these "levees" or, as she sometimes terms them, "receptions" appear to have been that one might never suspect her of having any commercial interest in them. All the same, money did change hands, and visitors like Ulysses S. Grant and the thousands of spectators who crowded to view her at Barnum's Museum before her marriage to Tom Thumb paid out additional money for the autographed photographs she sold.

Following her wedding to Tom Thumb and the formation of the General Tom Thumb Company—whose principal members originally consisted of Lavinia and her sister Minnie, Tom Thumb and Commodore Nutt, and their manager Sylvester Bleeker—the same sort of program established earlier for Tom Thumb's entertainments was closely adhered to. The General continued to give his impersonations (his growing portliness, however, eventually led him to give up some of them, together with the "Grecian Statues"); Lavinia and her sister sang in their childish treble voices; the Commodore danced and engaged in wisecracks with the other members of the troupe and their full-sized manager, who appeared onstage to emphasize their diminutive stature; a comic piece usually rounded out the bill. The stage, as before, was set with miniature furniture, and the small ponies used to draw the diminutive carriage in which the company rode to and from their places of exhibition were carefully loaded aboard trains and boats and went at the same rate as regular passengers. The same pattern of publicity and entertainments was employed by Lavinia until the end of her career—long after the other members of the original "quartette" had departed this life—and there are people still living who can recall seeing, and excitedly running after, the tiny carriage in which Lavinia and her second husband Count Primo Magri rolled up to the doors of halls and theatres in their towns.[2]

Sometime around the turn of the century Lavinia decided to commit her memories to paper, and the result was the manuscript that is here finally published. The precise wanderings of this document following Lavinia's death are unknown, but it is believed to have been sold at the auction of her effects in 1920. Eventually it was acquired by the New Haven bookseller C. E. H. Whitlock from Leonard M. Robinson of Vineyard Haven, Massachusetts. The next and final purchaser was the author Alice Curtis Desmond, who made some use of the manuscript while writing her children's book *Barnum Presents: General Tom Thumb* and then presented it to the New-York Historical Society in 1953.[3] With the exception of a few excerpts used by Mrs. Desmond and the published portions discussed in the Appendix, Lavinia's autobiography is here presented for the first time.

Lavinia's manuscript, consisting of a total of 229 numbered leaves plus numerous attached slips of varying lengths, appears to have been composed during two different periods and may be said to constitute two distinct drafts. The first, written in fine, normal-sized characters, from a reference to Queen Victoria at the beginning of chapter 9 would seem to have been composed, or at least begun, before that monarch's death in 1901. It is conceivable it was commenced much earlier than this, possibly a few years after Tom Thumb's death in 1883, but additional evidence leads me to believe it was indeed written around 1901. In a letter to an acquaintance dated 5 November of that year, for example, Lavinia, in answer to a request for information about Tom Thumb, writes as though she were then working on or had recently completed the manuscript: "I have no biography of the Genl. My own autobiography I hope to have published and put out to the public before long."[4]

12

The revised or second draft was apparently made a few years later, around the time Lavinia succeeded in placing portions of her autobiography in the Sunday Magazine section of the fall 1906 issues of the *New York Tribune* (see the Appendix) and no doubt was entertaining hopes of shortly seeing the whole of her story in book form. At this time a few marginal notes concerning the location of illustrations (photographs Lavinia possessed) were added; occasional directions to the compositor, evidently in the hand of an editor, were also inserted; and at the point in chapter 5 where Lavinia relates the tedious tale of the "white African" she pinned a note of her own to the manuscript: "This story of the 'White African' contains about 1000 words. If you choose to cut it out, keep it intact & return to me, that I may use it elsewhere." The additional handwriting in this draft is not so fine as formerly (though this was likely caused by the use of a different pen) and on those original leaves where corrections were made is sometimes in backhand to distinguish it from the earlier writing. Other corrections and additions made at this time were written or typed on new leaves, or else on slips which were either pinned to or pasted onto the original leaves. It is evident the typed passages do not constitute a distinct third state in the evolution of the manuscript, and in a few instances they themselves have been corrected or replaced by handwritten passages in the second style.

These additional typed or handwritten leaves and slips were all incorporated into the original manuscript, the majority of whose leaves were therefore preserved, allowing us to follow—often with interesting results—Lavinia's fashioning of her autobiography. When not actually pasted onto the original leaves, their locations were indicated through the use of symbols, although a few such additions, as is mentioned below, are evidently out of place.

It must be acknowledged that Lavinia took several shortcuts while writing her memoirs, in which she sometimes quotes, generally without attribution, passages from Barnum's own autobiography and the pamphlets describing her and Tom Thumb. Most notable of all, in the latter part of the manuscript, is the wholesale lifting of material from Sylvester Bleeker's *Gen. Tom Thumb's Three Years' Tour around the World*, published in 1872, the year the company returned to America. No doubt Lavinia's memory, at the distance of thirty years, required some prodding, and the temptation to plagiarize from her former manager's highly readable account obviously proved irresistible. It is a pity she did not provide us with more

13

of her own descriptions and impressions in these chapters, the majority of whose incidents are to be found in Bleeker's book. Still, these chapters do contain a highly informative and, for the most part, interesting account of the company's tour through the American West and the Orient. For this reason I have decided to let them stand, crediting Bleeker (as will be seen on the title page of the present publication) with his proper share in the work. Readers wishing to ascertain for themselves the extent of Lavinia's foraging, or to read an even fuller account of the three years' tour, are directed to this writer's book.

As will be seen in this half of the autobiography and in earlier chapters, Bleeker himself played no small part in the fortunes of Lavinia, her husband, and their diminutive troupe. A former actor and stage manager who had made his debut at Mitchell's New York Olympic Theatre in 1842, he later became prompter at the theatre in Barnum's Museum and professionally assisted his employer on several occasions prior to assuming the management of the General Tom Thumb Company. He was, without doubt, a man of great resourcefulness and business acumen, and he obviously enjoyed the full confidence of Barnum and Lavinia. At the time he wrote his narrative of the tour around the world (a work no doubt undertaken at Barnum's behest, for the book was copyrighted in his name), he had been in Barnum's service for twenty-three years and was proud to dedicate his book to his "kind employer and sincere friend." As Lavinia writes, their grand tour excited even more curiosity about them among the general public, and Bleeker's book, we may be certain, experienced a brisk sale "on the show" once the troupe resumed their travels in America.

Nor can the reader of these memoirs ever forget, always hovering somewhere in the background, the commanding presence of P. T. Barnum. Fifty-two years old when Lavinia entered his service, he was to remain her friend and mentor until his death in 1891; and he was also the silent partner of Lavinia, her husband, and Bleeker in their tours until, feeling he was of no more use "than a fifth wheel to a coach," he generously resigned his interest to them in 1876. If he does not appear to have contributed much during the many years of this partnership, it must be remembered that it was through his masterful understanding and practice of advertising and publicity that Lavinia, Tom Thumb, and the other "little people" who joined

14

him at his American Museum first rose to prominence. It was also Barnum who played a key role in Tom Thumb and Lavinia's courtship (a famous description of which—supposedly submitted to Lavinia, Tom Thumb, and the rejected suitor Commodore Nutt for their approval—appears in his autobiography) and who, after reaping a windfall from the publicity surrounding their forthcoming union, finally managed to check his money-making propensities long enough to give them as decorous a wedding as he could. Such uncharacteristic restraint did not, of course, inhibit him in his subsequent promotion of the famous little couple.

Fortunately, there is no scarcity of illustrations to chronicle Lavinia's and Tom Thumb's progress over the years. Hundreds of different photographs, it would seem, were taken during their lifetimes, many of them in the small *carte de visite* format, photographed by such masters as Mathew Brady (one of whose studios was across the street from Barnum's Museum) and sold by the thousands to spectators at the conclusion of their entertainments. Even the death of Tom Thumb became the indirect topic of one studio photograph depicting a pensive Lavinia in her widow's weeds. Lavinia herself was an avid collector of photographs, and her albums, several of which are in the New-York Historical Society and the Bridgeport Public Library, contain many fascinating prints of herself and her contemporaries. The majority of these are studio portraits, but there are other less formal photographs, taken of Lavinia in later life, that show her outdoors. Standing stiffly amid bucolic settings, with trees, an occasional house, or normal-sized people in her vicinity, she seems even more diminutive than in the studio portraits with their gigantic-looking furniture, somehow estranged from, even threatened by, her natural surroundings. A haunting, almost surrealistic photograph—tinted, for some reason, a deep blue—in the Bridgeport Public Library depicts a distant Lavinia alone in a wheat field, the wheat rising nearly to her chin. In another photograph of her and her second husband Count Magri at a country fair, taken a few years before her death, a stout and wrinkled Lavinia stares beyond the gaping spectators crowding around their tiny cart—resolute, as one imagines from the last chapter of her autobiography, in her belief that she "belonged" to the public and could do no better than to remain on show until the very end.

These evocative images of Lavinia serve as a fitting complement to her autobiography, in which so much is said that reveals her personality, prejudices, and general opinions, but so many other things are left unsaid. Her innermost feelings she keeps to herself, although at times, as when she writes about the deaths of her sister Minnie and husband Tom Thumb, the cheerful persona she presented to her public seems in imminent danger of slipping. What did it mean to her, one wonders, to finally realize that, unlike her classmates at the school in Middleboro, she would never attain normal size? How did her parents react to this seeming calamity? And what were her feelings upon first hearing applied to herself the terrifying word "dwarf"?—a term Lavinia herself, it will be noted, is everywhere careful to avoid, but which journalists, Barnum, and the public in general continued to use in describing her, as well as all the other "little people" with whom she worked, until the very end of her life. The Arabs, she writes in describing the visit of the General Tom Thumb Company to view the Pyramids, stared at them on their donkeys and broke into "shouts of merriment," and they themselves joined in the laugh. Did the perpetual joke of her littleness ever pall for Lavinia? And did she never sense, on the part of some spectators, at least, a streak of cruelty in this laughter?

She must have, of course, but there is scant indication of such awareness in the autobiography itself. There she is consistently depicted—as no doubt she was—as a brave little trooper, determined to prove that in both mental and physical capacity she was fully the equal of normal-sized persons. On her reverses in later life she is also silent, although it is apparent from other sources that the immense sums of money earned by her and Tom Thumb, the jewels they amassed (described by a nephew as the largest private collection in America[5]), Tom Thumb's fleet horses, yacht, and extensive properties in Bridgeport all eventually slipped through their hands—whether from prodigality and poor management, as is often claimed, or owing to the financial climate of the time is difficult to say. Certain it is that as early as 1878 Lavinia was writing to her friend Barnum, pleading for his aid to establish a museum:

> If you remember, when General and I were at your house last time we spoke to you about starting a museum. We have been talking it over and we think if you would help us in the way of money we could settle for the winter, as Mr. Bleeker will

manage for us commencing before the holidays. Mr. Bleeker could get a good party and give a lively first-class entertainment—we could get our living and make a little something. If you do not wish to have it known that you are helping, it is a secret. I do hope you will give this a serious thought for several reasons: one is General must have excitement and that would be quite enough, and it is very hard for me to travel every day or two, although Mr. Bleeker is very kind and makes the journeys short as he can. I know times are hard, but now is the time for you to lend a helping hand to those that are worthy. Perhaps after a time we would get established so that we would never travel again. The country is full of little people, but the times are hard. Yet we make enough to keep up, but I dread the cold so much.[6]

But the fatiguing travels continued, and the subsequent years do not appear to have been any better. Following the death of Tom Thumb in 1883 and Lavinia's marriage to Count Primo Magri two years later—a marriage, her nephew writes, that was not a happy one, for in private life the Count was "the exact opposite of Tom Thumb"[7]—the wealth and possessions of former days continued to disappear. The Middleboro home built by Tom Thumb after their three-year tour around the world was let; the jewels adorning the silver horse and chariot presented by Tiffany's at Lavinia's first wedding were replaced by paste gems and sold; other gifts, articles of virtu, and miniature furnishings were sold piece by piece to help make ends meet.[8] Although ever aware of her duty to appear fashionably dressed before her public, Lavinia now ordered most of her gowns from American, rather than Parisian, dressmakers; the Count, in order to save money, took to riding through the streets of Middleboro on a specially built bicycle. Meanwhile, they and their small troupe continued to tour, presenting their entertainments in halls, museums, and vaudeville theatres. An undated broadside in the New-York Historical Society advertising them at the Grand Museum in New York City refers to Lavinia, the Count, and his brother Baron Ernesto Magri as the "Lilliputian Atoms" and "Diminutive Trio." Another undated document—this time a program printed at Exeter, New Hampshire—gives a clearer idea of what their entertainments were like. Following an overture and an introduction by the Countess Magri, a "Professor" Logrenia, formerly of the Crystal Palace, Sydenham, and the Royal Polytechnic Institute, performed feats of prestidigitation. Then followed a brief comedy entitled *Two Strings to Her Bow, or Which Will Win Her*, with Lavinia as the Beloved, the Count as the Lover, and the Baron as the Unfortunate Lover. After an intermission of five minutes the Professor returned to exhibit a trained bird act, and the entertainment concluded with a patriotic levitation number called "Astarte," somewhat ambiguously described as follows: "Sleeping in mid air, by the Countess and Logrenia. While suspended in the air, the Countess will be placed in different positions and dressed in costumes to represent several different characters, concluding with THE GODDESS OF LIBERTY." [9]

There is something irresistibly funny in contemplating Lavinia, stout and sixtyish, in the role of an ingenue (though the feat has often been attempted in the legitimate theatre, to be sure), yet it was one in which she evidently felt at home. A printed playlet by Robert Griffin Morris entitled *A Peep at Mars*, copyrighted in Lavinia's name, was obviously written expressly for the company and bears the information that it was first produced at Springfield, Massachusetts, on 18 March 1901. [10] The cast is limited to the three characters of the Lady, the General, and Pharaoh—the last two identified in the directions as the Count and the Baron, respectively. In the course of the action, which is set on Mars, the Lady flirts with the other two, and Pharaoh whistles an accompaniment to the General's singing "The Last Rose of Summer."

In the new century Lavinia continued to tour until almost the time of her death. And while she was now signing herself on her souvenir photographs and other documents as the "Countess M. Lavinia Magri," almost always—such was the magic of the name—she added the information "Mrs. Genl. Tom Thumb" beneath. In her entertainments as well she continued to trade on her former husband's name. Writing to her brother Benjamin from Hartford on 9 September 1915, she noted that the hot weather and competition from a local fair were keeping some patrons away, "yet I think the company will get their share of business, the old name still draws the crowd (Mrs. General Tom Thumb)." [11] The company also performed in a few movies around this time; and for a while, during the summer months, Lavinia and the Count exhibited themselves at Coney Island, where they were photographed for a colored postcard standing outside what was supposed to be their residence in "Midget City, Dreamland." In their last years they also ran a small general store known as "Primo's Pastime" near their home in Middleboro, where patrons could purchase photographs of them.

On 25 November 1919, at the age of seventy-eight, Lavinia died at her home in Massachusetts after a long illness. Five days later, while a light rain was falling, her body, encased in a grey coffin, was lowered into a tiny grave next to Tom Thumb's in Bridgeport's Mountain Grove Cemetery. The Count had accompanied the body from Middleboro, and a large crowd of mourners from the circus and theatrical professions turned out to pay final homage to the little lady whom the *Bridgeport Post* described as "one of the world's most famous dwarfs."[12] Although Lavinia had expressed the wish that what remained of her possessions might be kept together and preserved in a museum, the Count, who planned to return to Italy with the proceeds, auctioned them off the following October. The amounts realized were disappointingly low: a miniature grand piano, a gift from Queen Victoria, brought only $11; the highest bid, for a canopied bed (probably the same now in the Barnum Museum), was $81.[13] Almost immediately the Count himself fell fatally ill and two weeks later, on 31 October, the anniversary of his wife's birth, died at Middleboro. He was buried there in St. Mary's Cemetery.

*   *   *   *   *

In preparing Lavinia's autobiography for publication, I have followed the corrected, second-draft state of the manuscript, mentioning any significant departures from the original in the notes. The only exception occurs in the "contents" at the heads of most chapters, which Lavinia crossed out while revising her narrative but which I have nonetheless retained as being of possible aid and interest to the reader. Since the original leaves of a few chapters containing these headings were discarded in the revision process, some of them have been lost. It will also be noted that such headings are not always complete for the chapters they describe, since new material added while Lavinia was making her revision—her later life with Count Magri, for example—is not mentioned in them.

Without wishing to meddle with the manuscript any more than

was necessary, I have everywhere retained Lavinia's syntax—dangling modifiers included—although on occasion, either through oversights on Lavinia's part or, in one instance, the loss of a corner of one leaf of the manuscript, I have supplied missing words within brackets. I have not felt compelled to follow her punctuation, however, and have freely changed this to bring it more into line with modern usage and to aid the reader in following Lavinia's sometimes convoluted sentence structure. In a few instances, too, I have pointed run-on sentences and have broken or melded excessively long or short paragraphs.

In the case of Lavinia's orthography, with the exception of a few obviously unintentional errors in those additions to the manuscript which are typewritten (an operation at which Lavinia was no expert), I have preserved the original spelling intact. It will be noted that I have generally supplied the notation "*sic*" following only the first instance of a misspelled word, although in a few cases I have found it more expeditious to supply missing letters within brackets. Nor have I thought it necessary to force a consistency upon those few words—"center/centre," "endeavor/endeavour," "employee/employe," etc.—for which Lavinia uses alternating spellings. In the latter part of the manuscript I have also followed the spelling Lavinia supplies for foreign place names. Capitalization has been regularized, and words that were broken in Lavinia's day have been joined or hyphenated to give them their modern forms. Where Lavinia quotes from Barnum and other writers, I have followed her manuscript and not her sources—although, as is indicated in a few of the notes, it is sometimes interesting to compare these passages with their originals, if only to learn what Lavinia omitted or thought advisable to change. Editorial comment within the text is printed in italics and bounded by brackets.

* * * * *

There remains but to thank those who have aided me in the preparation of Lavinia's autobiography, in particular Mr. James Gregory, Librarian of the New-York Historical Society, who encouraged me in my plans to publish the manuscript and presented my proposal before the Library Committee of the Board of Trustees. The permission of this body to publish the manuscript is gratefully acknowledged. I must also thank Mr. David W. Palmquist, Head of Historical Collections at the Bridgeport Public Library, and his assistant Miss Barbara Strong for their generous help; and Mr. Robert Pelton, Curator of the Barnum Museum in Bridgeport, who kindly searched out and made available to me materials at his institution.

THE AUTOBIOGRAPHY

of

Mrs. Tom Thumb

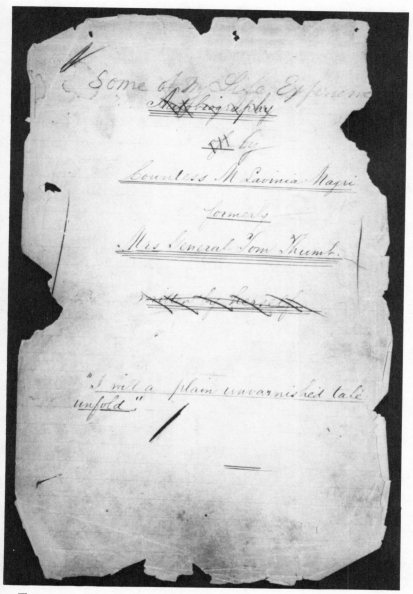

Some of My Life Experiences

~~Autobiography~~

~~by~~

Countess M. Lavinia Magri

Formerly

Mrs General Tom Thumb.

~~by herself~~

"I will a plain unvarnished tale
unfold"

THE TITLE PAGE, WITH CORRECTIONS, TO THE COUNTESS M. LAVINIA
MAGRI'S AUTOBIOGRAPHY

To the memory of my

Father and Mother,

to whom I owe a happy childhood and whose
integrity and uprightness has given me a
standard which, if often my arrow falls
below, has held me to the motto
"Aim high."

Preface

IT IS SAID THAT EVERY PERSON making their advent upon this earth has an appointed mission to perform.

I never imagined that I had an especial "mission" to write a book, but having been so frequently solicited to "write the story of my life," not only by friends but by various publishers, the thought was suggested that perhaps some occult power was at work conspiring to make me do the deed—impressing on my mind that such was my mission.

Seriously, however, I have felt that my public life and experiences have been so varied and in a sense unusual; my travel so extensive, embracing Europe, Asia, Australia, Africa and America; my association with many of the most prominent personages in this and foreign countries so intimate; and my career so full of incident that my autobiography might be both interesting and amusing.

It has been asserted of General Tom Thumb that he had kissed more ladies than any living man. I can with equal assurance assert that I have *shaken hands* with more human beings, royal and plebeian, rich and poor, great and small, old and young, native and foreign, than any other woman in existance [*sic*]. I do not say this boastfully but only to show how large has been my experience for the years I have been before the public.

I have endeavored to adhere strictly to facts, and if the personal pronoun appears rather prominently, it is to be remembered that in telling one's own story that seems necessary.

If the reading of this my life history prove acceptable, it will be a source of gratification to me.

COUNTESS MERCY LAVINIA MAGRI,
better known as Mrs. General Tom Thumb,
Middleboro, Massachusetts

Chapter 1

A FEW CURIOUS IDEAS REGARDING MY BIRTH, PARENTAGE AND
ANCESTRY. A MAN OF THEORY. A SUPPOSED RELATIONSHIP.
MY BIRTH AND DESCRIPTION OF MY FAMILY. AN OVER-
ZEALOUS MISSIONARY. MY SCHOOL DAYS. A GLEEFUL BUT
DANGEROUS RIDE. AS A SCHOOL TEACHER.

DURING MY LONG AND EVENTFUL public career there has ever been
earnest inquiry by nearly all with whom I have come in contact at
my receptions and entertainments as to my birthplace, parentage,
ancestors, habits etc., my country visitors especially asking "Whar
was you raised?" as if I were a rare plant or a curious quadruped. "Be
the rest of your folks as little as you be?" is a common question. One
old lady, upon being introduced, raised her hands in wonder and
surprise and exclaimed, "Land o' goodness! you air a little mite,"
then giving me a critical gaze, added, "It can't cost much for yer
board. I don't s'pose you eat anything but spoon vittles." Perhaps
hotel keepers could answer that supposition quite as well as I.

At one of my evening receptions a man who had listened
attentively during my conversation with several ladies at length
beckoned my manager (Mr. Bleeker) aside and pointing to me asked
whether "that little person had good common sense?"—not a very

31

flattering estimate of my conversational powers. "Yes," replied Mr. B., "that little lady has common and *un*common sense. I have observed you listening to her conversation for several minutes—cannot you judge for yourself?" "Well, yes," he replied, "I did listen, but I have heard that Barnum has something to do with this affair and I know what a humbug he is; you can't believe your own eyes and ears where he is concerned. Those ladies may be in collusion with him and their dialogue arranged and taught her for the purpose of deceiving the public. My theory is antagonistic to the claim that she does possess common sense." "What is your theory?" inquired Mr. B. "First," said he, "I argue from the sound premise that intellect depends upon the size of the brain, the larger the brain the larger the intellect; secondly, the growth and size of the head depends upon the size and strength of the body. If the body be small it cannot supply the necessary physical requirements to increase the size of the head: therefore, a small head is the result of a small body, a small brain is the result of a small head and a small intellect is the result of a small brain. Hence, *she* having a small body has a small head; having a small head she has a small brain; having a small brain she has little sense or intellect. I have made the subject a deep study and my conclusion is perfect."[1] Mr. Bleeker, recalling Solomon's advice to "answer a fool according to his folly," replied, "As I understand you, a man having a head as large as a bushel knows more than one whose head would fit in a peck measure." "Well," said he, "a-hem! yes, that's about it; rather quaintly expressed, but you have caught the idea." "Ah!" said Mr. B., "I now see the great error Mr. Barnum made a short time ago. He advertised for a man to act as manager for his Museum, inserting as a necessary requisite for the position 'brains wanted as well as hands.' He experimented with merchants, lawyers, physicians and even clergymen, but failed to find a capable person. It is certain he would not have been subjected to so many disappointments had he known and adopted your theory and picked out from his curiosities the largest-headed giant or fat man in his collection. Write to Mr. Barnum, my dear sir, explain your theory as lucidly as you have to me, and he will heartily thank you for giving him such an excellent guide for the future." "I will do so! I will do so!" he replied. "Good evening sir, good evening"—and glancing pityingly at me he walked out of the hall fully convinced that I did *not* possess "good common sense."

LAVINIA AS A YOUNG GIRL. THE SIGNATURE WAS PROBABLY A LATER ADDITION.

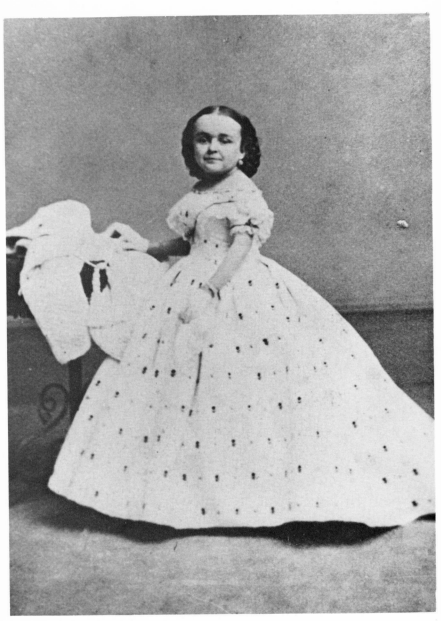

LAVINIA AS A YOUNG WOMAN

P. T. Barnum admiring one of his "curiosities," the dancer Ernestine de Faiber. Published by Mathew B. Brady. This photograph may be a fabrication by Brady, who specialized in "composite" photographs, but is nonetheless interesting as a comment on what was rumored to be a strong affinity between the showman and the lady.

"The Fairy Wedding Group," depicting Commodore Nutt, Tom Thumb, Lavinia, and her sister Minnie Warren

"GEN. TOM THUMB, WIFE & CHILD." ANOTHER OF BARNUM'S HOAXES

Minnie Warren and Commodore Nutt in his uniform

"The Lilliputian Card Party," depicting, from left to right, Lavinia, Commodore Nutt, Minnie Warren, and Tom Thumb. Note the small settee in the foreground.

Tom Thumb, Lavinia, Minnie Warren, and their manager Sylvester Bleeker

One day a loquacious old gentleman introduced himself with the remark, "I think you and I are related; my name like your own is Warren. I can trace my lineage back over 200 years. I thought I would call and ascertain whether we were not of the same blood." I bowed for him to proceed and he continued. "In 1650 three brothers of the name of Warren settled near Plymouth in Massachusetts: they were christened Richard, Peter and Stephen. Richard, the eldest, was lame and had a humpback; he was usually called Richard 3d. Peter, the next eldest, had remarkably large ears—he was a smart fellow—the folks nicknamed him 'Donkey Warren.' The youngest brother, Stephen, had six fingers upon one hand. I am a descendent [*sic*] of his. He was a baker and supplied the settlers with bread. He marked his bread by impressing his hand with the six fingers on every loaf. His bread was known as 'the six-finger Warren loaf.' There is a very remarkable fact connected with the descendents of those brothers. In Richard's line there is always in each family of every successive generation one member who limps and has a humpback; in Peter's line one member with very large ears; and in Stephen's line one who has either six fingers on one hand or six toes on one foot." I remained silent. After a moment's thought he hesitatingly inquired, "Has any—er—er—of your family six fingers or six toes on hand or foot?" "No," I replied, "to my positive knowledge they neither limp, are humpbacked, have very large ears or have six fingers or six toes. It is quite evident that my branch never grew on your geneological [*sic*] tree." "I am very sorry, very sorry," exclaimed the old gentleman, closely eyeing my hands and feet, then bowing and bidding me "good day" retired with a much disappointed air.

In recalling this incident I am reminded that I have not enlightened my readers regarding my ancestry. The name of Warren is well known both in England and America. The Warrens of America occupy conspicuous positions in our country's history: among them James Warren, John Warren and General Joseph Warren, who laid down his life for his country at the battle of Bunker Hill. As the loquacious old gentleman would say, I am "of Gen. Joseph Warren's blood."

I trace my pedigree directly back through Richard Warren of the Mayflower Company to Reginald de Warren, son of William, Earl of Warren, and his wife Isobel, daughter of Hugh "the Great."

William senior, Earl of Warren, married Gundreda, daughter of "William the Conquer[or]." He took his title from the town of Warren in Normandy. He died in England in 1088, which is as far back as I have traced my ancestry, but I fancy this is sufficient to prove my (English and) American nationality.

I was born October 31st, 1841, on the old Warren farm in the town of Middleboro, Plymouth Co., Mass. Had I possessed the power I would not have chosen any other place wherein to make my first appearance on this globe to anxious and admiring attendants. The atmosphere pervading the localities made famous in our country's history no doubt imparted to me many characteristics—amongst them my intense patriotism. My entrance into the family circle had been preceded by two male and two female children and was followed by two male and one female—all of whom were above the ordinary stature except the youngest named Minnie, who was born June 2d, 1849. She was of the same stature as myself and after my marriage accompanied me on my trip around the world and shared most of my experiences till the time of her death [on] July 23d, 1878. My father was nearly six feet tall and my mother was termed "a large woman."

They have both passed on, before me! Their lives were proverbial for a high standard of integrity, morality and charity. I cannot better express my estimate of their character than to say that they faithfully fulfilled the "two great commandments, upon which hang all the law and the prophets."

I remember frequently hearing the remark applied to my father by our neighbors while I was yet too young to comprehend its import, "James is a merciful man," but when I became older I learned to fully understand its meaning when I read the words "A merciful man is merciful to his beast"—for early and late, hot and cold, sunshine and storm, his cattle always received his personal care and attention, upon which errand I often accompanied him. Even after I had arrived at years of maturity, it was one of his great pleasures to take Minnie and myself one upon each arm and make the rounds of the stable and barns.

34

Both of my parents for 50 years were consistent members of the "Church upon the Green" over which presided the Rev. Dr. I. W. Putnam. All of the family were expected to attend divine service every Sunday morning, and no persons were prouder of their children than my parents when we were all seated with demure mien in the large family pew. The younger children were compelled to attend the Sabbath school at the conclusion of the church service. I mention this fact as a matter of information for those of my readers who may have entertained the opinion that I had not received a proper religious training in my youth, as once [was] expressed to me at one of my public levees by an over-zealous female worker in the Lord's Vineyard. Pushing her way through the throng surrounding me, she exclaimed in a high-toned voice, "Miss Warren, I have a message for you." I was somewhat startled at the announcement, my fears conjuring up the thought of some calamity to my family. "From whom?" I inquired. "From the Lord," said she, and handed me a tract; then she continued, "Read and heed it. Here you are wasting your life in this vain and frivolous manner, puffed up with pride and vanity, adorning your person with finery and gee-gaws" (*she* was dressed in the heigth [*sic*] of fashion) "and fondly receiving all this flattery and adulation and never giving one thought to your Creator. Your parents must be very worldly and wicked people to permit it. Probably they have brought you up in total ignorance of the Bible. What a terrible sin they have to answer for; truly 'vanity! vanity! sayeth the preacher, all is vanity!'" The ladies and gentlemen surrounding me gave audible utterance to such expressions as "What a shame," "The woman is insane," "I wonder some one don't remove her" etc. Although I knew she was carried away by her religious zeal, the imputation upon my parents whom I dearly loved incensed me and I could not resist the inclination to reply. Turning to her, I said, "In the proverbs of Solomon there is a passage which reads 'A fool uttereth his mind but a wise man keepeth it in till afterward'; another, 'Be not hasty in thy speech.' You charge my parents with being worldly and wicked. In early life, in the words of St. Paul, they 'put on the whole armor of God, girding their loins with truth, having on the breastplate of righteousness, taking the shield of faith, the helmet of salvation and the sword of the spirit'; therefore apply the words to yourself which you will find in Ecclesiastes, 'Be not rash with thy mouth and let not thine heart be hasty to utter anything.'" She gazed at me in open-mouthed wonder at my aptitude in quoting scriptures. I had studied these quotations in my Sunday school lessons. I continued, "The same preacher also said, 'There is a time for everything, a time to weep and a time to laugh, a

35

time to *get* and a time to lose, a time to mourn and a time to dance, a time to *keep silence* and a time to *speak*,' and if the 'preacher' were here now, no doubt he would tell you that the time to approach me with such language as you have uttered is when I have retired to the privacy of my hotel." When she had recovered from her confusion, she stammered out as she edged away, "I—I—beg pardon— I—I—I didn't intend to offend you," and speedily retreated from the hall.

Reader, pardon this digression. To return to my infancy. When the ceremony of "weighing the baby" was completed it was announced that I tipped the scales at six pounds. Until I was a year old I was of the usual size; from that time I increased in stature very slowly, not growing in five years as much as an ordinary child would in one. I continued growing at that rate until I was ten years of age and then ceased entirely. At that time I was twenty-four inches in heigth and weighed twenty pounds. I attended school with other children in our neighborhood and found no difficulty whatever in keeping up with them in my studies. At home my dear mother taught me to sew, knit, cook and do all manner of housework, so that I really became an excellent housekeeper. To overcome the inconvenience of my diminutive stature my father constructed for my use a pair of light portable steps which I could readily handle and standing upon which I could easily reach the topmost shelves in the closets. I also acquired a knowledge of embroidery and other fancy work. I went to school like other girls, but being fond of fun and having in common with most children the idea that fun consisted in doing mischief, I fear that my teachers didn't wholly appreciate me from that standpoint. One of my usual pranks was to run about under the desk and administer surreptitious pinches to the unconscious children; and they, startled by the unexpected attack, would suddenly scream. It is to be remembered that in country schoolhouses of that day there was one continuous desk around the outside of the room against the wall, and thus, my size enabling me to walk readily under it, I could make the circuit of the room without coming out from under cover. The teacher—Mr. Dunbar—knew at once the cause of the uneasiness and outcry, and would promptly start in pursuit; but I had the advantage for I could readily see him and easily dodge, while he had as much difficulty in locating me as if he were *It* in a game of hunt the slipper. Watching my opportunity,

36

I'd dart back to my seat, and when he rose, red and panting from an ineffectual search under the desk, he'd find me demurely poring over my lesson as if I'd never had a thought outside my book. Here my size was in my favor. The teacher being a great strong man, his instinctive chivalry wouldn't let him strike a feminine mite like myself and in dire desperation he'd exclaim, "What shall I do with you! Shall I shut you up in my overshoe?"—he had enormous feet—"What does your mother do to punish you? Does she set you on top of the sugar bowl and make you wipe the dishes?"

For the time being I was conquered, for any allusion to my abnormal size always caused me great embarrassment, and the helpless man had really no other weapon to turn on me. Later, when a teacher myself, I appreciated his position, but my repentance came too late to be of any benefit to him. In all my wide experience in later years I've always felt profound gratitude for my New England birth and education.

It was the custom of the woodenware, tin-pan, and broom peddlers, when they made their tour through our section, to stop at our house for dinner, the fame of my mother's New England boiled dinner being known amongst the fraternity. Even Mr. Barnum, who presumably lived on the fat of the land, was fond of it; and for many years after we were connected in business, whenever he intended to visit us, he would telegraph the day he was coming and add, "Tell your mother to have a New England boiled dinner for me." The peddlers didn't telegraph but managed to get here about dinner time and take their chances. So upon one occasion while the peddler was dining with the family and Minnie and I were playing outside the house, I suggested to Minnie that it would be a good chance to take a ride. Minnie was seven years my junior and at that time no higher than my shoulder; by climbing, pushing, tugging and pulling, I succeeded in getting with her upon the seat of the waggon. I suppose we looked like two dolls placed there for sale. Putting my arm around Minnie, I took hold of the lines which being too large for my hand gave me really no control over the horse. Fortunately the animal was gentle and, having traveled the road frequently, knew all the turns. I spoke to him and off he started. The noise of the wheels attracted the attention of the folks in the house, but by the time they reached the door we were rattling down the hill. It required my utmost strength to retain my hold upon Minnie and cling to the seat, and it was a wonder we were not thrown upon the road. One of my brothers ran to the stable, led out a horse, and mounting bareback started in pursuit. When overtaken, we were over a mile upon the road to town and going at a lively trot—for I continually urged the horse forward by calling "get up! go 'long!"—the tin and wooden-ware rattling and banging behind us. We were in high glee, laughing and enjoying the fun, but my brother took us back and I received a long lecture upon the danger I had incurred, and a promise was exacted from me never to do the like act again. The peddler, after examining his wares and finding no damage, treated the matter as a good joke, saying "I have owned that horse for 12 years and the greatest speed I could get out of him was three miles an hour, but I now believe the animal is a racer." Since that time I have become an expert horsewoman and until within a few years have always kept horses for my individual driving.

When I was sixteen years of age the district school had become so large, it was decided to divide it and form a primary department consisting of scholars between the ages of four and nine years. The school committee waited upon my parents and through them offered me the position of teacher. I accepted, and at the re-opening of the school I was duly installed in my new undertaking. I was very zealous in my duty, and at the end of the term I received the commendation and thanks of the committee for the excellent discipline I maintained as well as the progress made by the pupils under my tuition. The youngest even was far above me in stature, yet all seemed anxious to be obedient and to please me.[2] When I had occasion to reprimand, it would be received with meekness and repentance. I thought I had now found a proper and genial vocation, but during the subsequent vacation an event occurred which entirely changed the tenor of my life.

Chapter 2

PORSPECTS OF A CHANGE IN LIFE. A FAMILY COUNCIL. DEPAR-
TURE FROM HOME. MY FIRST APPEARANCE IN PUBLIC. LIFE ON
THE WESTERN RIVERS. A GIANTESS. A BIG BABY. BATTLE
WITH THE ROUGHS; ANOTHER WITH THE "RED SHIRTS."
MEETING WITH ULYSSES S. GRANT, THE CITIZEN. ALMOST A
FATAL ILLNESS. INTERVIEW WITH HON. STEPHEN A. DOUG-
LAS. SECESSION MEETINGS AND MURMURS OF WAR. HASTEN-
ING HOME.

MY FIRST APPEARANCE as a public character came as a surprise to the
home, for up to that time no one had thought of such a thing. But a
visit from a cousin of ours changed my life current.[3] He was by
profession manager of a museum in the days when a museum meant
a great deal to the general public. I had some idea of what a city
museum was: staid, stuffy and wearisome, visited by everybody that
was anybody and all the nobodies as well. But this museum was a
novelty, a "floating palace of curiosities" on the Ohio and Mississippi
rivers. The prospect of travel, the going "out West" as we then called
it, the novelty of a sail on the beautiful Ohio—La Belle River [*sic*], as
the early French settlers named it—and on the mighty Mississippi,
with all the glamor which youth throws about the unknown, made

me eager to go, and I added my entreaties to his when he broached the subject to my parents and begged to be allowed to take me with him. After a rather stormy family session, during which my eldest brother declared that if I was allowed to go he would leave the house forever, my parents gave a reluctant consent, binding Mr. Wood by solemn promise to keep me under his personal supervision and cousinly care. Early the next morning I left home with Mr. Wood, who was far too wise to take any risks of a reconsideration, and we went to his parents' home in Weedsport, New York.

They were lovely old people, and their kindness, tenderness and cheerful good nature left me no room for homesickness while I waited for Mr. Wood to go to Cincinnati where the boats were lying to prepare for the season's work. When at last all was ready, Mr. Wood, whom his men always called "Colonel" though I never learned why, came for me; and thus began my public life in April 1858 when, to quote one of Mr. Wood's statements advanced to influence my parents, I was to "gain a world-wide reputation." Of the results none of us could have had any premonition.

The Colonel owned a floating theatre, minstrel hall and museum, combined upon one large boat which was towed by a smaller steamer wherever it was desirable. This tow-steamer was commanded by Captain Tucker, who afterward became prominent as a Confederate officer during the Civil War. These boats traversed the Illinois, Ohio, Mississippi and Missouri rivers their entire navigable lengths, stopping at all the river towns on the route. Board and accommodations were furnished upon the steamer.

To those unacquainted with the western rivers it will be well to explain that our "show" was on one of the regular boats used in those waters. Owing to the uncertainty of the river's volume, which might be very "low" in dry weather or might be very "high" in spring or after heavy rains, stationary wharves could not be used, but at each landing was a "wharf-boat" which, rising and falling with the river, offered always a wharf on a level with the boat's lower deck.

These steamboats, being flat-bottomed—a deep draught boat would have been useless—have all their machinery on the lower deck, and thus the "saloon" above reaches the whole length of the boat, from bow to stern. As will be seen, this gave a clear view the full length of the boat, affording opportunity for a stage etc., and the staterooms on either side were excellently planned for retiring rooms. These staterooms had a door opening on "the guards," forming a sort of back door so the performers could pass to the stern of the boat and enter the saloon at the rear, instead of passing through the audience. In that respect they were more convenient than our eastern boats.

This peculiarity—it seems such to our eastern ideas of steamboats—of having the machinery on the lower deck, with the furnaces in front, gave them at night a particularly wierd [*sic*] appearance. When the furnace doors were thrown open, dark figures could be seen passing back and forth in front of them, tossing in wood and coal which, blazing up, added to the strange glare, while high above long streamers of dense inky smoke, not infrequently enlivened with sharp tongues of flame or glittering fiery sparks, trailed behind from the tops of tall smokestacks. The general appearance was startling, especially to one brought up in the orthodox faith. My father used to tell the story of an old woman who, when she first saw a locomotive whizz past her front door, described it as "hell in a harness." When I first looked into the bow of one of these boats at night, I thought they'd left off the harness.

Among the curiosities in the museum department on the boat was a "giantess" nearly eight feet tall from Wilton, Maine. Mr. Wood assigned me to the stateroom occupied by Miss Hardy and in a measure placed me under her care. I looked at her with awe, something such as Jack the Giant Killer may have felt in his first acquaintance with those big people of childhood's imagination. I had never seen such a gigantic being before, and my heart failed me at the thought that I was to be almost continually in her company. When she removed her shoes, I gazed at them in wonder. They were even more cavernous than the overshoes I remembered with such dread as one of the terrors of my school days. However, she spoke to me affectionately, and I was with her but a very short time when I learned to love her and to realize that her great body was quite a necessity if it was to contain her large heart. If I felt tired or was suffering from severe headache, to which I was subject, she would lift me upon her expansive lap and soon soothe me to sleep. Looking back to it now, I realize that we must have made a comical combination, and I sometimes wonder whether we shall look the same in heaven, to which she passed many years ago but where I confidently expect to meet her.

41

In the minstrel company were several members who afterward became very popular in their profession and whose names are well known in that line in every city in the Union. One of them was "Billy Birch," who was established for many years on Broadway, N.Y., under the firm name of Birch, Backus, Bernard and Wambold's San Francisco Minstrels.[4] Mr. Birch was almost entirely bald, and as he would lie in his room of a warm summer afternoon, his head resting upon a pillow in the window, enjoying the cool breeze, it looked so smooth and so like an enormous infant's head that he received the appellation of "the baby." Even his wife, who accompanied him, always spoke of him as "her baby." If she visited us in our room, she would usually remark, as she arose to leave, "Well, I must go and see what mischief my baby is doing."

In advertising the "show," handbills were sent ahead and distributed in the towns along our route, announcing the date of our arrival. We would invariable [sic] find a large crowd awaiting to board our boats. In some of the southern states the license [fee] was so extremely high—there being in fact three licenses: state, county and town—that there would be but a small margin of profit. The state license once paid covered the state, the county license was twice as much as the state, and the town license twice as much as the county. If there had been two or three more licenses at this rate of geometrical progression, all amusements would have been effectually shut out. To avoid the town license, which was the heaviest, Col. Wood would receive the audience on board, sail up or down the river until beyond the jurisdiction of the town, give the entertainment, then return to the town and land the people.

In those years there was usually a rough element in almost every town, who considered that there had been no fun without "a fight with the showmen" as a finale. Although strict orders had been given to every employe to avoid in every manner possible any collision, it seemed often impossible, even with the greatest caution, to escape it; consequently, such troubles were of frequent occurrance [sic], and as firearms were freely used, we were in constant fear. Upon one occasion several of the minstrels after the evening performance went ashore to view the town. While walking quietly along, they met a party of roughs who endeavoured to pick a quarrel with them and finally attacked them. Our men fought their way clear and ran for the boat, pursued by the yelling mob; they succeeded in getting on board and hoisting the landing gangway, and were thus safe for the time from further molestation. As we had but a short run to the next town, the intention had been to defer starting until ten o'clock the next morning; but Col. Wood, knowing that the trouble had not ended, ordered steam up by six o'clock. Early as it was, we were awakened by a howling, yelling mob on the levee, armed with guns and pistols, demanding that the "showman [sic] come ashore and fight it out." No attention being paid to them, they became exasperated and opened a fusilade upon the boat with stones and firearms.

As these missels [sic] were not discriminating, we non-combatants were in as much danger as anybody. Our terror soon increased, for the angry mob hurridly [sic] secured planks and there was every indication that they would be successful in their design to come on board the boat. To our great joy, at that moment the engines began to move and slowly but surely the boat drew away, dropping the ends of their boards into the river, and the infuriated leaders found their ardor cooled by an involuntary ducking in the coffee-colored water. Someone on shore took deliberate aim and fired at our pilot, but the bullet passing through his hat lodged in the roof of the pilot house, where we let it remain as a trophy. Before he could fire again, our increasing speed put us out of danger from such inhospitable messengers. They then gave us a parting volley, which our boys answered with derisive shouts.

At Stillwater, Minnesota, a great lumber country, the lumbermen came down the river from their camps on rafts to visit us. Known throughout that country as "Red Shirts," they were a terror to peace-loving people. Eager to fight, they did not always wait for a good reason, but "pitched in," as they expressed it, for pure love of fighting. They did not slight us, but after a lively half hour they scuttled back to their rafts. No one on our boat was seriously wounded, for they were under cover, but as firearms were freely used it was considered quite probable that some of the Red Shirts would cut no more lumber that season.[5] Considering discretion the better part of valor, we chose the better part and left the locality before daylight next morning.

It cannot be denied that these occurrences were a little disquieting. I was travelling, as I had wished. I was seeing the world, as I also had wished, but this particular phase of it wasn't exactly

43

anticipated in my early dreams and could have been dispensed with without serious regret. I learned, however, to regard these troubles with less terror and finally treated them philosophically.

On our first trip up the Mississippi we stopped at Galena and remained there three days, and there I first had the pleasure of meeting with General Grant. He was then a private citizen in business in the town. He came to the museum, having read a description of me published in the press of the places we had visited. He became very much interested and conversed with me for some time, and having purchased my photograph, asked me to put my autograph upon it, which I did. The next day he returned with his family and introduced them to me; they would not enter the performing hall, but remained conversing with me. They departed with expressed pleasure at our meeting and many good wishes for my welfare. I afterward met the General while in active service during the Civil War, and also while filling the high office of President. An account of which I will give later.

My naturally strong constitution withstood for a long time the influence of the many low malarial localities which I necessarily visited, but at last I was stricken with a slow fever; and although I had the best medical attendance to be obtained in the towns we visited, it finally developed into a severe case of typhoid. For nearly three months I hovered in a condition between life and death. It was then that Mrs. Lizzie Edmunds, wife of Morris Edmunds, one of the minstrel performers, showed her unselfish devotion. Every moment not applied to her duties she gave to me. Placing me upon a pillow, at night through the weary hours she would hold me upon her lap, intently watching my every move, bathing my face and moistening my parched lips. At length a change came and I began slowly to recover, but it was several months before I was able to stand the fatigue of an exhibition.

In the fall of 1860, during the Presidential campaign, I met the Hon. Stephen A. Douglas at Montgomery, Ala., where he made a formal call upon me. Shortly after, we met again at Selma; he sent his card to me and I received him in my reception room at the hotel. He expressed great pleasure at again seeing me, and as I stood before him he took my hand and, drawing me toward him, stooped to kiss me. I instinctively drew back, feeling my face suffused with blushes. It seemed impossible to make people at first understand that I was

44

not a child; that being a woman I had the womanly instinct of shrinking from a form of familiarity which in the case of a child of my size would have been as natural as it was permissable [*sic*]. With the quick perception that was a part of his nature, Mr. Douglass [*sic*] understood, and laughing heartily, he said with a merry twinkle of the eye, "I am often called 'the little Giant,' but if I am a giant I am not necessarily an ogre and will not eat you, although you almost tempt me to do so." After a pleasant chat he took his leave with many good wishes for my prosperity and happiness and that I might "never again be frightened by a giant."

We continued our journeyings until after the election in 1860, when the doubts, fears and excitements which preceded the coming storm of our civil war were being everywhere felt. We were then in the lower Mississippi states, where the people were holding most excited secession meetings. Northerners were looked upon with suspicion; our business fell off and there seemed small chance for any improvement—there were graver matters to take public attention. Every available craft on the river was being appropriated for transportation use. The prospect of being stranded in an enemy's country was not exhilerating [*sic*].

Colonel Wood decided that the most prudent course was to dispose of the boats and take his company north as speedily as possible. He succeeded in selling the boats, and they afterwards did service for the Confederacy. Ascertaining that there was a steamer then *en route* for Louisville—the last one going north for the season—and there being a possible chance of intercepting her at Vicksburg, we took the first train for that point. Already the railroads were being used for the carrying of munitions of war from point to point, and travel by them was very uncertain. After many delays upon the road, we reached Vicksburg on the morning of December 2d. The steamer had landed about two hours earlier and was then discharging and taking on freight preparatory to sailing again at 3 P.M. The hotel was crowded with people awaiting an opportunity to go north.

Mr. Wood hastened to the agents of the boat, only to be told that the boat was already overcrowded and not another passenger would be taken. He then went to the captain and pleaded with him, but the captain very naturally refused to go against the agents' orders. In despair Mr. Wood then urged the captain to call upon me that I

45

might receive the refusal from his own lips, thinking possibly that when he saw me it might influence his decision. To this the captain at length consented, and returned to the hotel with Mr. Wood and was introduced to me. Whether my size did more for me than my tongue I never knew, and didn't feel disposed to question, so long as the exceedingly desirable result was obtained.

After a short interview the captain turned to Mr. Wood and said, "If you will quietly and speedily get your people to my boat, I will resign my cabin to Miss Warren and the other ladies; the rest must accommodate themselves as best they can on the deck." His offer was eagerly accepted, and when we were seated in the carriage we realized the necessity for haste and caution when we saw our "cash-box" come flying through the window. Our agent, being obliged to walk, felt the danger of carrying it openly, and so after our carriage was in motion threw it through the window to insure its safety. The driver appreciated a U.S. greenback as much as if he were not "secesh," and within an hour we were safely on board the boat.

After a pleasant passage, no incident occurring worthy of note, we landed at Louisville. Accompanied by Mr. Wood, I took the earliest train for my home in Middleboro, where I was received with great demonstrations of joy by my parents and family, who knowing that I had been in the South had felt some little anxiety concerning my immediate return. After a recuperative rest I went to my friends in Weedsport, and between these two "homes" I spent the next eighteen months except [for] an occasional trip to fill engagements at county and state fairs, which proved a source of profit to Mr. Wood and gave me glimpses of a quiet country life quite unlike the exciting scenes of previous months.

It was from here that I went to Syracuse and was allowed to visit the detention cells in the courthouse. It was my first experience in that line, and I could not rid my young heart of the feeling that it was cruel to lock these people in those cells. I gave no thought to the wrong they had done and that this was the only way our clumsy justice knew. I could think only of the personality of the individual. The interest they showed in me and the gentleness with which they spoke to me seemed, to my ignorance, fair tests of their character. Later in life, when knowledge of the world and its wickedness had grown, I looked on English prisons and even the gloomy dungeons of Italy and the Inquisatorial [*sic*] chambers of Venice with less feeling of wonder-sympathy than stirred my childish heart then. Auburn and Sing Sing seem all right to me now. Till we can do better and eliminate causes, we can only deal with effects as seems best to our present knowledge.

Chapter 3

A NEW FIELD OF ACTION. PROPOSITION FROM MR. BARNUM.
MY ENGAGEMENT WITH HIM. RECEPTION AT THE ST.
NICHOLAS HOTEL, N.Y. OPINIONS OF THE PRESS. RECEP-
TION AT THE PARKER HOUSE, BOSTON. NEW YEAR CALLS AT
THE 5TH AVE. HOTEL, N.Y. INTERVIEW WITH GENERAL
WINFIELD SCOTT.

I DOUBT WHETHER MR. WOOD really had faith in his prophecy that "I
would gain a world-wide reputation" when he painted my future in
such glowing colors to gain my parents' consent to permit me to go
upon exhibition, but during this period, from certain indications, he
began to have glimpses of its possibility and, realizing the value to
him of my increasing popularity, used every endeavor to keep me
under his control.

During the summer of 1862, Mr. Barnum, having heard of me
through the western and southern press and also having received
verbal accounts from those who had seen and conversed with me,
and thinking there was a possible opportunity of duplicating the
great pecuniary success which had attended his introduction to the
public of the famous Genl. Tom Thumb, sent an agent to Middleboro to see and interview me. Being satisfied with the report of the

agent, he again sent him to my home to open negotiations with my parents for my appearance at his Museum,[6] corner of Broadway and Ann St., New York, to be followed by a tour of Europe. From the first I strenuously opposed the proposition, not fully appreciating the opportunities offered me for fame, fortune and an enlarged knowledge of the world, which I had ever eagerly craved. I entertained a deep sense of gratitude for Mr. Wood's kindness to me, and gratitude is a strong feature in my character. I considered that *he* should reap a goodly share of the benefit accruing from any prominence I may have attained, he having been the first to introduce me to my new sphere of action upon life's stage. I had also observed a betrayal of worry and anxiety on his part through fear that he might be deprived of this benefit, and my feelings were strongly enlisted in his behalf; but who can control fate! My parents and family favored the new road presented for me to follow, the only deterring obstacle being an erroneous impression of Mr. Barnum's character, whom they looked upon as an arrant "humbug." They thought he would do something to lead the public to think there was some deception in me—that I should be looked upon as another of Barnum's "humbugs."[7] In fact, my parents confessed such ideas to the agent. That the agent so interpreted them was made quite evident a few days after his departure, for Mr. Barnum sent an invitation to us to visit him at Bridgeport. I little thought when we accepted that invitation how many important events would quickly follow and be crowded into my life's history, one of the most important and least anticipated being my marriage almost at the opening of my career. I had heard of General Tom Thumb and seen him once, but knew nothing of his character, reputation and fame.[8] I was destined, however, shortly to know and marry him, thus fulfilling the adage "the unexpected always happens." I was first introduced to the General a few weeks prior to my visit to Mr. Barnum. Mr. Barnum in his autobiography states that I first saw and was introduced to the General while I was given [*sic*] levees at the Museum, but he was in error. I will quote from Mr. Barnum's autobiography published in 1872, giving an account of my first business connection with him as follows:

> In 1862 I heard of an extraordinary little woman named Lavinia Warren who was residing with her parents at Middleboro, Mass., and I sent an invitation to her and her

parents to visit me at Bridgeport. They came and I found her to be a most intelligent and refined young lady, well educated and an accomplished, beautiful and perfectly developed woman in miniature. I succeeded in making an engagement with her for several years, during which she contracted to visit Great Britain, France and other foreign lands. Having arranged the terms of her engagement, I took her to the home of one of my daughters in New York while I was procuring her wardrobe and jewelry and making arrangements for her début. As yet nothing had been said in the papers about the interesting young lady.[9]

When my wardrobe was completed, Mr. Barnum engaged rooms at the St. Nicholas Hotel and extended an invitation to the members of the press to attend a reception given by me. The following are a few of the many notices given by them, nearly all written in the same complimentary vein. I disclaim all vanity in offering to my readers these "opinions" so flattering in their tone. If nature endowed me with any superior personal attraction, it was compa[ra]tively small compensation for the inconvenience, trouble and annoyance imposed upon me by my diminutive stature.

[*At this point in the manuscript Lavinia has pasted in a clipping from a promotional pamphlet,*[10] *containing the opinions of writers for the* New York Tribune, Times, *and* Sun, *followed by a hand-copied account from the* Commercial Advertiser. *Since the writers' comments often touch on Lavinia's appearance and physical attributes—of which she was justifiably proud—the editor has thought it best to retain several of them.*]

Opinions of the Press

The *N. Y. Tribune*, of Dec. 23, 1862, says of her: "Yesterday we saw a very pretty and intelligent little lady at the St. Nicholas Hotel, in this city. This woman in miniature is 21 years of age, weighs 29 pounds, and measures 32 inches in height. She enjoys excellent health—has a symmetrical form, and a perfect physical development. She has a full, round, dimpled face, and her fine black eyes fairly sparkle when she becomes interested in conversation. She moves about the drawing-room with the grace and dignity of a queen, and yet she is entirely devoid of affectation, is modest and lady-like in her deportment. Her voice is soft and sweet, and she sings excellently well. . . . "

The *New York Times*, of same date, says: "We attended Miss Warren's reception yesterday at the St. Nicholas. It was a festive gathering. All were paying court to a very beautiful, an exceedingly symmetrical, a remarkably well-developed, and an absolutely choice specimen of feminine humanity, whose silken tresses beautified and adorned a head, the top of which was not quite thirty-two inches from the floor. In other words, we saw a miniature woman—aye, and the queen of them. Her face is bright and sweet, her eyes brilliant and intelligent, her form faultless, and her manner that of the woman of the world. What more could we desire?"

The *New York Commercial Advertiser* says: "We found Miss Warren to be one of the most extraordinary little ladies at any time seen in this age of extraordinary beings. She is . . . beautifully developed in physical form and has great mental aptitude. Her size is so small that a baby-chair is quite large enough for her to sit upon. She has dark, rich, waving hair, large, brilliant and intelligent eyes, and an exquisitely modeled neck and shoulders. Her bust would be a study for a sculptor, and the symetry [*sic*] of her form is such that were she of the average size she would be one of the handsomest of women."

Mr. Barnum wished me to give levees at his Museum, but he had agreed in his contract that I should make my first appearance in England [as] soon as my wardrobe was completed. I was therefore greatly annoyed when he urged the request upon me. The following is my reply to his note offering me one thousand dollars per week to do so:

St. Nicholas Hotel, Dec. 26th, 1862

P. T. Barnum, Esq. Dear Sir,

In reply to your note of this morning, I beg to say that in consequence of Messrs. Ball & Black not being able to complete all the jewels ordered for me, my departure for London will be delayed a week or two. I, however, visit Boston, as arranged, tomorrow and as I do not contemplate giving public exhibitions until I have appeared, as per contract, before the Courts of Europe, I must respectfully decline your offer.

Your obedient Servant,
Lavinia Warren

I left immediately for Boston and gave two receptions at the Parker House to the elite of the city. One day was devoted to Governor Andrews and suite. While in Boston I agreed to Mr. Barnum's proposition. The following from the *Boston Transcript* explains itself:

BARNUM VS. QUEEN VICTORIA.—THE SHOWMAN VICTORIOUS.—The indefatigable Barnum, who in vain offered the miniature lady, Miss Lavinia Warren, a thousand dollars per week for public exhibition, it seems was determined not to give it up so. The little lady arrived at the Parker House Monday night. Barnum arrived at the Winthrop House Tuesday morning. It now appears that the showman came by the way of Middleboro', where he found the parents of Miss Warren, and induced them to accompany him to Boston. Having probably plied them with *golden* arguments, he called a family council yesterday (the little Queen, of course, presiding), and after a lengthy debate, which was resumed in the evening, the *petite* aspirant for the honors of foreign courts yielded, and forthwith a treaty was drawn and signed by the high contracting parties, by which it was stipulated that the sovereigns of America (the sovereign people) shall be permitted to attend the public levees of their citizen Queen, at such times and places, for the space of three or four weeks, as Mr. Barnum shall provide. At the conclusion of this engagement, little Miss Warren will start for the Courts of Europe with a few extra thousands in her pocket.[11]

Returning from Boston, I arrived at the Fifth Avenue Hotel Dec. 30th, 1862, and on New Years Day, January 1st, 1863, received "New Years Calls." Among my callers were many who afterward became famous, among them Generals McClellan, Burnside, Rosencrans and McPherson. I remember I found myself looking on them as they came before me in full uniform as something quite apart from ordinary life, though I little dreamed how long the terrible war would last or how rapidly these smiling gentlemen were making history. General Winfield Scott was at that time at the hotel, confined to his room by illness, and he sent to ask me to call on him. Accompanied by my secretary, I went to his room. As I entered, he extended his hand and drew me gently toward him. I was quite awed as I stood near him and realized that within that massive frame which reposed on a reclining chair was the soul of the man I had been taught to regard as next to George Washington. To stand there with my hand in his and hear him speak so gently, he whose brain had guided armies to victory and whose voice had thrilled soldiers to deeds of bravery, seemed like a dream from which I should wake to find my hero worship was but a passing shadow. With the fine perception of his grand nature, I think he read my thought; and kindly bidding me be seated, he began to talk of ordinary things, asking after my family, my early life and other topics upon which I was soon talking freely and naturally. As I was about to leave, he called the servant to bring wine, and pouring it with his own hand, he gave me a glass and lifting another to his lips said, "I wish you a Happy New Year, and I thank you for coming to see me when I was unable to come to you." As I thanked him for the season's compliments, I added that I hoped to hear soon that he was quite recovered and that he might long be spared to serve the country that needed him so much. It seemed as if a shade of sadness crossed his face as laying his hand tenderly on my head, he said, "God bless you, my child, for your good wishes." It was the only time I ever saw this truly great man, but the interview is vividly impressed on my memory, and I've always felt glad that it was my privilege to see him in the quiet of his own room and thus get a glimpse of the softer side of his giant heart.

Other callers, of much less interest to me, however, were the Vanderbilts, Astors and others of the "Four Hundred," though that term had not then come into general use and very surely the number of my callers was not limited by that fanciful term. I remember with vivid pleasure a call from Mrs. James Gorden Bennet [*sic*], whose subsequent experience with brigands in Italy will be remembered.[12]

Chapter 4

LEVEES AT BARNUM'S MUSEUM, N.Y. ENGAGEMENT AND
MARRIAGE WITH CHARLES S. STRATTON (GEN. TOM THUMB).
DESCRIPTION OF CEREMONY. DRESSES, BRIDAL GIFTS ETC.
CORRESPONDENCE BETWEEN MR. W—— S—— AND REVD.
DR. TAYLOR. ATTEMPTED BLACKMAIL. RECEPTION IN
PHILADELPHIA. VISIT TO THE WHITE HOUSE BY INVITATION
OF PRESIDENT LINCOLN AND WIFE.

JANUARY 2D, 1863, I commenced giving levees at Mr. Barnum's
Museum. I again quote from Mr. Barnum:

> At the time I engaged Miss Warren, Gen. Tom Thumb had
> no engagement with me and in fact he was not on exhibition
> at the time at all; he was taking a vacation at his home in
> Bridgeport. Whenever he came to New York he naturally
> called upon his old friend at the Museum. While Lavinia was
> giving her levees, the General came to the City and was at the
> Museum daily; of course they had many opportunities of
> being in each other's company. One day he came to my
> private office and desired to see me alone. I complied, but
> without the remotest suspicion as to his object. He first
> questioned me—which let in the light upon me—about

55

Lavinia's parents and family. I stated the facts, which I clearly perceived gave him satisfaction of a peculiar sort. He then said with great frankness and no less earnestness, "You have always been a friend of mine and I want you to say a good word for me to Miss Warren. I have plenty of money and I want to settle down in life." I told the General that this was too sudden an affair, that he must take time to think of it, but he insisted that years of thought would make no difference for his mind was fully made up. "Well, General," I replied, "I will not oppose you in your suit, but you must do your own courting. Miss Warren is no fool and you will have to proceed very cautiously if you can succeed in winning her affections." The General thanked me and promised to be very discreet. At his request I invited Lavinia to accompany me to Bridgeport the following Saturday and remain until Monday. The General met us at the depot in Bridgeport and drove us to my house in his own carriage. After visiting awhile at "Lindencroft" (my residence) he took Lavinia out for a ride, stopping at his mother's house. She there saw the apartment which his father had built expressly for him and filled with the most gorgeous furniture, all corresponding to his diminutive size. [*Here Lavinia inserts a footnote of her own*: I am still using the same furniture in my own home.] Then he took her to East Bridgeport and no doubt pointed out in detail all the houses he and I owned; they returned to lunch. I asked her how she liked her ride. She replied, "It was very pleasant, but it seems as if you and Tom Thumb owned about all of Bridgeport." The General returned with his mother at 5 o'clock for dinner. The next evening, Sunday, the General called and after spending a pleasant half hour asked me to step into another room and there announced, under promise of secrecy for the present, his engagement to Miss Warren. The next morning he brought a very nicely written letter which he wished to send to Lavinia's mother. He deputed his friend Mr. George A. Wells to be the bearer and receive the reply. On Wednesday Mr. Wells returned, saying that at first Mrs. Warren objected, for she feared it was a contrivance to get her daughter married for the promotion of some pecuniary advantage to me, but hearing from Mr.

Wells that in case of the marriage I would cancel all claim upon her daughter's services, Mrs. Warren consented.[13]

In 1861 Mr. Barnum had engaged a bright intelligent little man named George Washington Morrison Nutt. He named him Commodore Nutt and exhibited him in the Museum as the "$30,000 Nutt."[14] During my levees at the Museum, Mr. Barnum learning that my sister Minnie, seven years my junior, was also of diminutive stature, induced me to send for her. My parents brought her to the city and Mr. B., being greatly pleased with the beauty of her sweet face and faultless form, immediately made a proposition for her engagement, to which my parents were willing to accede as she would be under my care and supervision. The idea had presented itself to Mr. Barnum that by re-engaging Genl. Tom Thumb he would be enabled, as he expressed it, "to present to the public a quartette of the most wonderful, intelligent and perfectly formed ladies and gentlemen in miniature the world ever produced." This idea was consummated after my marriage; and as a preliminary, that the public might have a glimpse of us together, when arrangements were made for the wedding Minnie was chosen as bridesmaid and [the] Commodore as groomsman.

I will now return to the events prior to the marriage as related by Mr. Barnum:

> Of course when the approaching marriage was announced it created an immense excitement. Lavinia['s] levees at the Museum were crowded to suffocation and her photographs were in great demand. For several weeks she sold more than three hundred dollars worth of her *cartes de visite* daily and the receipts at the Museum were over three thousand dollars per day. I engaged the General to exhibit and assist her in the sale of her photographs, to which his own picture was added. I could therefore afford to give them a fine wedding and I did so.[15]

Mr. Barnum frankly confesses that the questions asked and the opposition raised in some quarters to this marriage became a source of pecuniary benefit to him by giving it such publicity that it increased the crowds at the Museum, and that because of this—which irreverent people might call free advertising—he tried to

57

defer the marriage and that he offered Mr. Stratton and myself fifteen thousand dollars to postpone our marriage for one month and continue the exhibitions at the Museum. As the General and myself were expecting to marry each other, and not Mr. Barnum, and as moreover we were neither of us marrying for money, we didn't quite see that a money offer was any part of the business, so we declined. Mr. Barnum further says that he had many applications for tickets of admission to the church to witness the ceremony, some offering as high as sixty dollars, but he refused it and not a single ticket was sold. Everybody in the church came by invitation, and thus the ceremony was conducted as would be any marriage of people less before the public. Whatever Mr. Barnum's peculiarities, he would not violate the wishes of friends or the sanctities of a church ceremony.

The following description of the ceremony, costumes, reception at the Metropolitan Hotel and bridal gifts is copied from *Frank Leslie's Journal*. A full description was also given in all of the daily journals; a repetition would be tedious.

[*The description mentioned is another long clipping pasted into the manuscript, detailing the* grand national event of the season *at Grace Church on 10 February 1863. To accommodate the diminutive bridal pair, a special platform with six small steps leading up to it was erected in front of the chancel. The Rev. Mr. Willey of Bridgeport, Tom Thumb's pastor, and the Rev. Dr. Taylor, rector of Grace Church, officiated, and the bride was given away by her own pastor, the Rev. Dr. Putnam of Middleboro. There followed a splendid afternoon reception at the Metropolitan Hotel, where pieces of the eighty-pound wedding cake were distributed to over two thousand guests and the profusion of gifts was displayed in a separate parlor, with the jewelry and silver thoughtfully secured under glass. In addition to a magnificent collection of jewels presented by Tom Thumb to his wife, there were gifts from such notables as Mrs. Cornelius Vanderbilt, Mrs. James Gordon Bennett, Mrs. Horace Greeley, Mr. and Mrs. Lennox, Mrs. Astor, and Mrs. Lincoln (a set of Chinese fire screens), while the firm of Tiffany and Co. bestowed a miniature silver horse and chariot ornamented with rubies, the Wheeler and*

Wilson Manufacturing Co. a miniature silver-plated sewing machine, and Barnum himself a curious singing bird-automaton, purchased in London, many years since, for one hundred pounds. *The festivities concluded at ten in the evening when the New York Excelsior Band formed in the street before the hotel and serenaded the bridal party. Lavinia and her husband then appeared on a balcony and were cheered by the dense throng of people below.*]

I will here close the description of my wedding, the reading of which no doubt has become to many of my readers rather tiresome, by the following correspondence, the only suppression being the name of the person who wrote to the Rev. Dr. Taylor and to whom Dr. Taylor's reply is addressed. It shows how a certain would-be witness to my marriage was not a witness—not having received an invitation—and so vented his spleen by asserting that he had been excluded from the use of his pew to which he had a legal right. I publish it as an admirable specimen of Dr. Taylor's courteous but strong logical reasoning, clearly defining the rights of a pew holder[16]:

> To the Rev. Dr. Taylor. Sir,
> The object of my unwillingly addressing you this note is to inquire what right you had to exclude myself and other owners of pews in Grace Church from entering it yesterday, enforced too by a cordon of police for that purpose. If my pew is not my property, I wish to know it; and if it is, I deny your right to prevent me occupying it whenever the church is open, even at a marriage of mountebanks, which I would not take the trouble to cross the street to witness.
>
> Respectfully your obedient Servant,
> W—— S——

[*The Rev. Dr. Taylor seems to have devoted most of the day to answering this irate parishioner, for his letter, though not without an abundance of wit, runs on for over four leaves of Lavinia's manuscript. Suffice it to say that the good*

*Doctor effectively demolishes W—— S——'s claim to any "property" rights
in his pew (though he does concede that, by the law of custom, W—— S——
is perfectly entitled to sleep in it during divine service, provided he does so*
noiselessly and never to the disturbance of your sleeping neighbors),
*and that he also expresses his surprise that W—— S—— should be so
disturbed over a* marriage of mountebanks *which, by his own admission,
he would* not take the trouble to cross the street to witness. *The
wedding, he concludes, was as* touchingly solemn as a wedding can
possibly be rendered *and was* most emphatically a high triumph of
Christian civilization.]

A curious attempt at blackmail was made upon Mr. Barnum
soon after my wedding.[17] A lady called upon him at the Museum
and showed him a little six-page pamphlet which she had written
entitled "Priest and Pigmies" and requested him to read it. He
glanced at the title and, estimating its character, threw it down,
declining to waste his time reading it. "You had better look at it, Mr.
Barnum," said she. "It deeply interests you and you may think it
worth while to buy it." "Certainly," said he, "I will buy it," and
handed her sixpence. "Oh, you quite misunderstand me," said she.
"I mean buy the copyright and the entire edition with a view of
suppressing the work. It says some frightful things, I assure you."
Mr. Barnum laughed heartily at this weak attempt at blackmail.
"But," persisted the lady, "suppose it says that your Museum and
Grace Church are all one—what then?" "My dear Madam," he
replied, "you may say whatever you please about me or my Museum—you may print a hundred thousand copies of a pamphlet
stating that I stole the whole communion service from the altar of
Grace Church or anything else you may choose to say; only have the
kindness to write something about me and then come to me, and I
will properly estimate the money value of your services as an advertising agent. Good morning, Madam," and she departed quite
crestfallen.

On the day succeeding the marriage we started on a bridal tour,
intending to visit Philadelphia, Baltimore, Washington and the resi-

dences of our respective parents in Connecticut and Massachusetts. The following from the *Philadelphia Ledger* describes our reception.

[This, too—another clipping which adds nothing new—the editor has thought safe to dispense with, although he has decided to retain the one below from the Washington Star *on account of its reference to President Lincoln.]*

From Philadelphia we proceeded to Washington and to Willards Hotel. The next day we received an invitation from President Lincoln and wife to visit them at the White House. The *Washington Star* gives the following account of it:

> Last evening, at eight o'clock, the little couple visited, by invitation, at the White House, and were introduced to the President, Mrs. Lincoln, Secretaries Chase, Stanton, Wells, Blair, and Usher, and Senator Wilson, Generals Butler and Clay, Hon. J. J. Crittenden, and many other gentlemen of distinction, nearly all of whom were accompanied by their families. The President, in the course of the evening, remarked to General Thumb that he had thrown him completely in the shade; that he (the General) was now the great center of attraction. Refreshments were served to the guests of the President and Mrs. Lincoln, which the little folks appeared to relish as much as any person present. . . .

Mr. and Mrs. Lincoln received us very cordially. When Mr. Lincoln stooped his towering form to greet us, there was a peculiarly quizzical expression in his eye which almost made me laugh outright. Knowing his predilection for story telling, I imagined he was about to utter something of a humorous nature, but he only said, with a genial smile, "Mrs. Stratton, I wish you much happiness in your union." After receiving the congratulations of all present, the President took our hands and led us to the sofa, lifted the General up and placed him at his left hand, while Mrs. Lincoln did the same service for me, placing me at her right; we were thus seated between

61

them. "Tad," the favorite son, stood beside his mother and, gazing at me a few moments and then looking at his father, said half audibly, "Mother, isn't it funny that father is so tall and Mr. and Mrs. Stratton are so little?" The President, overhearing the remark, replied, "My boy, it is because Dame Nature sometimes delights in doing funny things; you need not seek for any other reason, for here you have the *long* and the *short* of it" (pointing to himself and the General). This created quite a laugh. A few minutes after, "Tad" again whispered to his mother, "Mother, if you were a little woman like Mrs. Stratton you would look just like her." This called forth the expression from several persons surrounding us that our forms and general appearance were much alike, a remark I afterwards frequently heard. "Mr. Stanton," said the President, "is Gen. Tom Thumb's name upon our army list?" "No," said Mr. Stanton; then turning to the General, inquired, "Where did you receive your title?" "From Queen Victoria," replied the General (this is a fact not generally known).[18] "Why, how was that?" asked Mr. Lincoln. "When I appeared before the Queen at Buckingham Palace," said the General, "there was present, beside the Queen, Prince Albert, the Prince of Wales, the Princess Royal (since Empress of Germany— they were children then), the Queen Dowager, the Duke of Wellington and a number of the nobility. Her Majesty called me to her and asked me a great many questions. As I stood by the Prince and Princess, I did not reach up more than a little above their waists. Mr. Barnum had introduced me as Tom Thumb. The Duke of Wellington remarked to one of the nobility, 'Their Royal Highnesses are head and shoulders taller than Tom Thumb.' Her Majesty heard it and turning to the old Duke said, '*General* Tom Thumb.' The Duke bowed and with a military salute to me repeated '*General* Tom Thumb,' and everybody bowed; after that I was always called by the title, and English soldiers always present arms as I pass." "You have never been called upon to do active duty in the field?" said Mr. Stanton. "Oh," quickly responded the President, "his duty now will always be required in the matrimonial field; he will serve with the home guard." We left the White House greatly pleased with our reception.

62

The next morning we received from the President a pass allowing us to cross the "Long Bridge" and a permit to visit the army camp on Arlington Heights. About one hundred and fifty thousand soldiers were concentrated there. Regiments were arriving and departing almost hourly. My brother Benjamin's regiment, the 40th Massachusetts, had fortunately arrived from the front the evening before, so we had a happy meeting with him. He was granted a furlough for a few days that he might accompany us north. As we rode through the vast camp we were greeted with cheers, throwing up of caps, and shouts from all sides such as "General, I saw you last down in Maine," "I saw you in Boston," "I saw you in Pennsylvania," "I saw you in old New York," "Three cheers for General Tom Thumb and his little wife," etc. etc. It seemed a joy to them to see a face which recalled to their minds memories of happy days at home. It was a grand but a sad sight to me. I reflected how many of those brave fellows would perhaps never again see home, wives or children, but their bodies, now so full of life, be lying inanimate on the battlefield.

Upon returning from Washington, we stopped at Baltimore; at New York, where a ball was given in our honor by Dodworth's band; at Bridgeport, where a reception was given us in the "Stratton home" which contained a ballroom 50 feet long; and from thence we went direct to Middleboro, where we were received by the "old folks at home" with every demonstration of good will. Immense crowds of the townspeople met us at the depot, escorted us to our dwelling and gave us a hearty New England welcome. It seemed to me, while resting in my quiet home after such a season of hurry and excitement, that I had just awakened from a strange dream. Scarce eight months had elapsed since I had departed from Middleboro in a calm and peaceful manner, but during that short period I had become a wife, had been welcomed and fêted by the highest personages both in public and private life, and had received a grand ovation from the inhabitants of my native town upon my return. Truly, it was a story from dreamland.

Chapter 5

PREPARATION FOR A TOUR THROUGH THE U.S. AN EXCITING
INCIDENT. NARRATIVE OF A WHITE AFRICAN. A PLEASANT
RIDE WITH GENL. GRANT. COL. FRED GRANT AS A BOY; HIS
AMUSING STORY OF A SPENT CANNONBALL. MILITARY WAITERS
AND A MILITARY ESCORT. NARROW ESCAPE DURING A RAID BY
GENERAL MORGAN IN KENTUCKY.

AFTER A BRIEF VISIT home we returned to New York, making our
headquarters at the St. Nicholas Hotel. It was the Waldorf Astoria
of those days, but would seem strangely behind the times to the
present-time traveller. Dinners and receptions galore were tendered
us.[19] With the latter I got on very well, for I was accustomed to
standing by the hour, but the full-dress, many-course dinners taxed
my patience even more than my digestion; and as it was at that time
the fashion to eat with gloves on, I found it rather inconvenient,
particularly as no gloves that fitted me could be bought but had to be
ordered, and I wondered sometimes whether the sky would fall if
the dealer failed to fill my order on time and I should find myself
without any that were clean enough to wear.

Again the date was set for our departure for Europe. It was to be
in October, and in the interim we were persuaded by Mr. Barnum to

give a series of levees at Irving Hall. Younger New Yorkers will ask where that was and will be surprised to be told it was at the corner of Irving Place and Fifteenth Street, and that it was considered at that time the most aristocratic place in the city. As Dan Bryant used to say in his minstrel show, "the place where the Big Bugs go!" Upon which the "end man" replied he'd rather go "where the bugs weren't so big."

These levees grew irksome to the General, and I was naturally anxious to go to Europe; so our combined entreaties had the desired effect and Mr. Barnum selected as his agent Mr. Sylvester Bleeker to go with us and arrange an entertainment which was to include General Tom Thumb and myself, together with Commodore Nutt and Minnie Warren. Mr. Bleeker himself appeared on the stage to accentuate the contrast between ourselves and people of normal size. This arrangement was so successful that Mr. Barnum asked that we fill in the time till October by a trip through New England and Canada.

We left New York for this trip on the last train that left the city before the tracks were torn up on the first morning of the draft riots. When we read of it in the papers, it was almost impossible to realize that the peaceful busy city we had left was in the possession of a raging mob and that from the lampposts were dangling bullet-riddled bodies of its helpless victims, that women and children were fleeing in terror and pale-faced men were hurridly closing their places of business. A reign of terror in our own New York seemed incredible. Houses looted, asylums burned and tracks torn up! Could these things be? The war was bad enough, but this seemed worse. One could think of soldiers fighting for a principle or enthused by a flag and encouraged by an idolized colonel, but here was cold-blooded treachery, murder and arson. Irresponsible men without leaders, following the blind instincts of brutal passions. And we had just escaped the horror of it!

Our train [was] the last to glide smoothly over the shining rails that reached out to the peace and restfulness of beautiful Stamford, where we rode under the spreading elms in blissful ignorance of the blood-thirsty cruelty we had left behind. We were without communication with New York for four days, and it seemed as if we were plunged in an oppressive stillness somewhere, where every nerve quivered with a desire for some sound to break the uncanny

65

silence. We went next to Norwalk, but I seem to have little memory of it. Every thought, every feeling was so absorbed by the knowledge that some unknown terror lay behind and the city from which we could get no message was in the throes of an undreamed of agony.

We also made a stay in New Haven. "City of the Elms," they call it, but I felt impelled to amend [this] to City of Noble Elms, for their majestic dignity might well demand a descriptive adjective. And the twin "Rocks" which guard its beauty are worthy of notice. "West Rock" is historically celebrated as a hiding place of "The Regicides." "East Rock" has since that time been made into a park, and from thence the view of the elm-embowered city must be fine. My heart rose in angry protest at the thought of these people sitting calmly down to let Hartford's energy wrest the capitol [*sic*] from them. Yet when we reached Hartford, I began to feel the same spirit of emulation and getting in touch with the people I understood.

With Springfield, Worcester and intermediate towns we were already familiar and our stops had no new interest. But an incident in Worcester was the culmination of a serious annoyance. Two men had followed us for some distance and we had been unpleasantly aware of their shadowing us. At Worcester, when our treasurer went to register for us, the two men stood near as if to observe him closely, and he said to the clerk in an undertone, "You have no rooms for these men!" The clerk was interested, and quietly sending for the police, the two men found themselves under arrest before they were aware that suspicion had been arroused [*sic*]. They confessed they had been following our party hoping for an opportunity to rob.

If modern methods of advertising had then been in vogue or yellow journalism, we should probably have been wise enough to have been interviewed and given out sensational stories of lost jewels etc. But I've a lamentable lack of imagination in such matters, and my New England training in early life developed in me a tendency to observe the limitations of facts.

Arriving in Boston, we gave our entertainments in Tremont Temple. The very walls seemed charged with the rampant patriotism of the time. Old Glory floated everywhere and draped every balcony. During our stay in Boston the General and myself visited the Charlestown Navy Yard and went on board several warships in the harbor. They say the cannon of the present day are much larger, but to us at that time those on the ships seemed gigantic. And so they were to us. When a midshipman lifted the General up to stand on one of them, he looked like "a little tin soldier" in comparison with it; and despite my terror lest he slip and fall, I felt a thrill of sympathy when he said, "This gun under my feet will help to bring the whole world to lay its tribute of respect at the feet of our goddess of republican liberty." The General's patriotism was sincere, and I'm glad he lived long enough to see his prophecy fulfilled.

From Boston we went toward Canada. The trip was uneventful save for an episode at Whitehall which lodged rather uncomfortably in my memory, vivid at first but gradually slipping into the mellowness of indifference. Our treasurer was as fond of fishing as our distinguished ex-President is said to be, and indeed he wasn't unlike him in figure; but I'm not sure that has any controlling influence over the choice of sports, though I've sometimes thought it might have. We were laid over on Sunday at Whitehall, and of course the man had to go fishing. So he came to me with our cash-box and asked me to become temporarily its custodian. I took it, placed it behind my trunk, threw some clothing over it and went to church, thinking no more of the box till the treasurer called for it. Then I went to bring it and lo! it wasn't there. At once there was a great commotion, for the box contained about $1,400 in cash and several government bonds. We all turned detectives and before long bagged the thief. Most of the money was found on the person of a chambermaid, who submitted with a very bad grace to the necessary search. But she would give no account of the box or bonds. A few hours later a boy picked up in a field a badly battered tin box containing papers, all of which he took to his father. Upon examination the gentleman discovered to whom they belonged and brought them to us. As we secured all but ten or twelve dollars and the poor girl was so thoroughly frightened and repentent [sic], we did not prosecute her and can only hope that our leniancy [sic] was not misplaced.[20]

As we heard no complaint of a scarcity of fish in Lake Champlain that season, we concluded our treasurer did not catch them all that day.

Reaching Quebec, we were invited to dine with Lord and Lady Monk at Government House, Lord Monk being at that time Governor-General of Canada, and accepted. I have a distinct memory of a long drive through beautiful grounds up to the mansion. Lord Monk was tall and stately, with dignified though genial manners. His "Lady" was as stately and greeted us with a gracious hospitality which put us entirely at ease. It was the first time I had seen servants in livery waiting on table, and I felt in more awe of the pompous butler than I was of his Lordship himself. Lady Monk walked out on the grounds with us, and I have even now some of the gorgeous autumn leaves she picked up for me and to which I have clung with a vivid remembrance of her graceful kindness. This fact of our invitation was sufficient to insure the attention of the elite of the Provinces.

To show how the quick thought and determined action of one person will check the fright and stampede of hundreds, I will relate an instance. The hall was crowded to overflowing [on] our opening night in Quebec. Across the hall, at the opposite end from and facing the stage, extended a deep gallery. Towards the end of our performance there was a sound of cracking timbers and the floor of the gallery suddenly settled down about two feet, the front balustrade retaining its position. Looking from the stage, the gap looked as if an enormous monster had opened its jaws. Those in the front seats downstairs observed it and, rising in a body, started with a rush for the doors; but as they would have to pass directly beneath the gallery to gain the exit, they hesitated a moment in fear. That hesitation, and the coolness and quick thought of Mr. Bleeker, saved many lives. Those in the gallery were either dazed or did not realize their danger. In a clear ringing voice, our manager shouted "Stop!" The tone seemed to strike and penetrate so sharply that they involuntarily turned their faces towards the stage. "Listen to me!" Not a person moved. He then continued in a distinct and measured tone, "A platform was erected in the gallery two feet above the floor to afford those in the gallery a better view of the stage; it has fallen to its level—nothing more." Then, with a quick motion bringing us forward, he said, "Our little people are desirous of giving you an opportunity of getting a near view and shaking hands with them: *follow my directions strictly*. To avoid confusion, those in the gallery will please retire *slowly* and *singly*, as the staircase is narrow, and fall in the rear of the line or pass out into the street; those here below will advance by the aisle at my right, pass across in front of the stage and make exit through this door at my left hand which leads to the street." The prospect of getting a near view of us seemed to have

68

obliterated from their minds the fright they had experienced; they moved forward as orderly as if leaving a church. An after-examination showed that the main girder supporting the gallery was broken in the centre and the ends partly torn from the walls. Had there been a violent motion such as would have accompanied a stampede, the entire gallery would have fallen. We closed for two days while repairs were being made and then concluded our engagement. Although we have had many experiences of alarmed audiences from breaking benches and cries of fire, Mr. B. has always succeeded in allaying the fears. After Quebec we visited Montreal, Ottawa, Toronto and the principal places in the Dominion.

The time for our departure for Europe was now near at hand, but we had received so many pressing invitations from all parts of the northern states to pay them a visit that Mr. Bleeker wrote an earnest letter to Mr. Barnum, urging a postponement of our departure for one year, saying that it would be throwing away the cream which an extended trip offered us. Mr. Barnum by return mail sent the following characteristic reply. "My dear Bleeker, Go on; save the cream. Your returns show it to be cream and not skim milk. Yours, P. T. Barnum."

We continued on our trip through the northern and western states. At Indianapolis, Major General Hunter came aboard the train and took a seat directly in front of us. After being seated a few moments he turned and, recognizing us, immediately arose and extended his hand. We conversed for some time, and although he was very courteous he impressed me as a reserved and very stern man. He was then on his way to supercede [sic] Frémont.

A remarkable story which sounded almost like a tale of fiction was related to us by a young man one day on the cars. He approached our seat and said to Mr. Bleeker, "May I have the privilege of conversing with these little people?" "Certainly," replied Mr. B., and offered him part of his seat. Said he, "I am a born African." As he was fair of complexion, we evinced some surprise. He laughed and said, "I do not mean to say that my parents were native Africans. General, I wanted to tell you that I saw your photograph in [the] possession of a native tribe in the unexplored interior of Africa." "How did it get there?" inquired the General. "I will tell you the story," he replied.

[Here Lavinia relates a long and rather tedious tale of a "white African"—a young man who had been born in the African bush of white parents captured by a native tribe after their ship had been wrecked. Remarkably, a photograph of Tom Thumb was salvaged from one of the seamen's chests, and the natives took a great fancy to it and seemed to understand that the General was a very little man. The photograph was carefully preserved and often shown to the "white African" while he was growing up, but was finally lost in a "war expedition."]

As we approached the depot at Columbus, Ohio, we saw the platform crowded with people and were informed that General Grant was to board the train on his way to Washington, having been called there to take command of the Army. A special car in which he rode was attached to our train. We had scarcely left the station when an orderly entered our car, advanced to our party and saluting the General said, "General Grant's compliments to General Tom Thumb and wife and would be happy to call upon them"; to which my husband replied, "Our compliments to General Grant and say we would be happy to receive him." The orderly saluted and departed. The grave formality with which the compliments were exchanged and the military attitude of the sedate orderly struck me as very comical, and I remarked to my husband, "I presume strict military etiquette must be observed when two great generals meet." Presently General Grant entered unattended, approached, shook hands and congratulated us. My husband resigned his seat next to me and insisted upon the General occupying it, which he did, my husband taking a seat beside Mr. Bleeker facing us. General Grant spoke of our first meeting at Galena, remarking that he still possessed my photograph with my autograph. He also told my husband when and where he first saw him. In the course of conversation he asked Mr. Bleeker "what points we intended visiting." Mr. B. said we had been on the borderline between the northern and southern states and he had been tempted several times to cross into the enemy's country, but had feared that we would not be allowed to pass our own lines. General Grant paused a moment, then spoke very slowly and meaningly. "Any person, unless a deserter from the Army, may openly drive a horse and buggy if they so wish through our lines without obstruction; when they have passed through, the other party will take care they don't return." We took it as a hint not to venture. After a pleasant chat he asked permission for his son "Fred" (now Colonel Fred Grant) to visit us. A few moments after the General retired, and soon "Fred" entered; he was a bright stalwart lad and very sociable. He told us he was with his father for some time during the Siege of Vicksburg and frequently accompanied him on reconnoitering expeditions. He said that General Grant at times appeared wholly indifferent to the fact that they were exposed to the enemy's fire, often drawn upon them by their close proximity to the works, but so long as he was with his father he had no fear. He told, in an amusing manner, of his own attempt to stop the progress of a spent cannonball. While standing beside his father, who was looking intently through his field glass, Fred saw a cannonball rolling along the ground apparently towards them; and in his boyish glee, it looked so innocent, he thought it would be fun to catch it and exhibit it as a trophy. He ran towards it, but he was startled by a loud shout from one of the officers who had happened to notice his intent. As he came to a dead halt, the ball sped by him at the rate apparently of forty miles an hour. "I was so surprised," said he, "that I looked in open-mouthed wonder at it. And what do you think?" he added. "My father, hearing the shout, merely looked around at me, then raised his glass and took no further notice. I thought he would scold me for being so foolish, but he said nothing until we were seated in the tent; then looking at me with a half smile, he merely remarked, "My son, never attempt to stop a spent cannonball; the chances are that it *will stop you*."

Upon our arrival at Wheeling we went to the McClure House. The hotel was overcrowded with military men who were hastening to Washington, summoned thence to join General Grant. They monopolized dining room, waiters and food; we could not obtain the slightest attention. The Commodore said he knew enough about war to know that foraging was allowable, so he rushed to the kitchen and, laying violent hands on a platter of fried ham, struggled back with it to the dining room. When he came staggering in under the weight of the huge platter, which however he couldn't reach to place on the table, the soldiers saw him and greeted him with shouts of laughter. Several of the officers sprang to his assistance. "I'm small," said the

Commodore, "but I've a grown-up appetite." Laughing again at his wit, some of them fastened their napkins about their waists and constituted themselves waiters, and rapidly transferred many dainty dishes from their own table to ours, even sending over champagne and wine and proposing the health of our party in contagious hilarity. It was a novel meal. After this event we had no further trouble in obtaining something to eat. When our little carriage came to the door to convey us to the hall, the officers with drawn swords formed an escort. They all attended our entertainment and at its conclusion escorted us back to the hotel, giving the General a military salute as we passed in.

Despite the hint we had received from General Grant, I was desirous of experiencing a little of the excitement attendant upon actual warfare and urged Mr. Bleeker to go into Kentucky. He consented, and we went to Louisville. The boats were being used as transports and were filled with blue-coated soldiers, but the glittering of friendly bayonets was attractive rather than formidable, whatever they may have proved to their antagonists, and obtaining the necessary permit, we embarked with them. We visited a camp of Rebel prisoners; they were well fed and appeared cheerful. Most of them had seen the General before and a few had seen me on the boat when I was traveling on the Ohio and Mississippi rivers, and so we became quite friendly. We also visited the earthworks which had been prepared in the suburbs of the city in anticipation of an attack. [John] Wilkes Booth, the assassin of President Lincoln, was at the time playing in Louisville. His room at the hotel was directly opposite mine, and he visited us several times. He expressed sympathy for the South, and his handsome face lighted [with] animation while conversing, but his language was mild and guarded. I thought very little about his expressed sentiments, for I had heard the same sympathy offered by numbers in the North, who received the name of "Copperheads"; in fact, two of our employees wore the Copperhead pin concealed under their coats. Booth presented me with his photograph, upon the back of which he wrote his name.

I will here take occasion to say that I was in London when President Lincoln was assassinated. The morning the news was received there, the proprietor of one of the London journals called upon me and asked if I had ever seen Booth and if so whether I would describe his appearance. I produced his photograph; the gentleman took it with avidity and at once offered fifty pounds if I would permit him to have a copy taken from it. I complied, and his was the first journal to publish Booth's likeness in England, so I thus aided the paper to get what American journalists call "a scoop." Upon the arrival of the first steamer from America, London was flooded with his pictures.

We visited Lexington, Frankfort, Bowling Green and all the cities and towns of note in Kentucky. At nearly every station on our route a detachment of soldiers would appear upon the platform as we approached and remain until our departure. Upon our arrival at a place named Paris, as we drove up to the hotel a body of Federal cavalry dashed up. The captain sprang from his horse, ran into the hotel, wrote a telegram, hastily remounted and galloped off with his troop. He was a splendid specimen of a cavalry officer, fully six feet two or three inches tall. His name, I ascertained, was Capt. Fitzgerald; he afterwards rose to the rank of general. News had been just received by him that a small town through which we had passed less than one hour before was then being raided by the Confederate General Morgan: the troop was off in hot pursuit. I thought it a lucky escape for us, and even then Minnie and I sat up half the night, afraid to go to bed, for like so many of the houses in that country [*sic*] our room did not communicate with any other, but opened immediately on an upper porch, from which stairs descended immediately to the lower. With our New England ideas of household interiors, it seemed much as if we were sleeping "all out doors."

We continued south until we were on the border of Tennessee; in truth, we had several times crossed the fighting line and deemed it prudent to return, particularly as our employes were in fear of being pressed into the Confederate service or, as General Grant expressed it, [that] "they upon the other side will take care that you do not get back again." On our return, when about the middle of the state, we were one day stopped with the information that General Morgan had, a few hours before, raided a town five miles ahead and had torn up the track for some distance and cut the telegraph wires. Word had been sent by a mounted courier to meet the train, which advanced slowly to the scene and had to remain there several hours until the track was sufficiently repaired for us to proceed. Another fortunate escape for us! There had been a skirmish between the raiders and the Union soldiers, in which the Union troops were successful.

73

Without further mishap we reached the state of Ohio and from thence continued our course to New York. We had been absent eleven months; and although our prices were low and our expenses were heavy, as we had a retinue of sixteen people together with a carriage and ponies, the trip yielded a nett [*sic*] profit of eighty-two thousand dollars.[21] This was certainly "pure cream and not skim milk."

Chapter 6

DEPARTURE FOR EUROPE. RECEPTION BY THE PRINCE AND
PRINCESS OF WALES. VISIT TO PARIS AND RECEPTION BY
EMPEROR NAPOLEON III, EMPRESS EUGENIE AND PRINCE
IMPERIAL. RETURN TO LONDON. RECEPTION BY HER
MAJESTY QUEEN VICTORIA AND ROYAL FAMILY AT WINDSOR
CASTLE. A COMPREHENSIVE DESCRIPTION OF ST. PAUL'S
CATHEDRAL, LONDON. DESCRIPTION OF OLD ST. PAUL'S.

OCTOBER 29TH, 1864, we sailed in the S. S. *City of Washington* for
England, our voyage occupying fourteen days. Think of that, ye
"Cookies"! Our anticipated arrival had been heralded far and wide,
and when we stepped ashore at Liverpool we were greeted by several
thousand people. Our carriage could make no progress through the
throng until a body of police forced a way for us. Indeed, the
General was more than once arrested for obstructing travel, but his
lawyer convinced the magistrate that as our carriage was a private
equipage, its owner could not be held responsible for the actions of
street gazers. On the strength of this decision, the General's sense of
fun led him perhaps to be a bit careless of the crowds. As he
expressed it, "Perhaps I drive about rather more than is necessary,
but these English draymen and the nobility's flunkeys all swearing at
my driver are amusing."

Sunday was "Mayor's Day," and the city was thronged with sight-seers to witness the procession, which is a gorgeous and stately affair conducted with all the pomp and decorum becoming the dignity of the Mayor's official position. Anxious to see the parade, we placed ourselves on the balcony, when to our dismay the waiting crowd, instead of parting to let the procession through, solidified in front of our window and halted the procession by mere force of their numbers, while they shouted and gazed not at the procession, but at us. We were obliged to go inside in order to make it possible for the procession, with its bands and military, its "Mace Bearers" and gorgeous attendants, to pass on. We were told that the Mayor felt some chagrin at being stopped and held an indefinite time by a counterattraction, but he certainly overlooked it, for later we were tendered a reception by him where we met his principle [sic] officials and the leading citizens of the city. We stopped at Linn's Waterloo Hotel, the same at which the General had stayed twenty years before.

Going from Liverpool directly to London, we were there summoned to Marlborough House to meet the Prince and Princess of Wales, like ourselves a newly married couple. [*A footnote inserted by Lavinia here points out that* I was married February 10th, 1863, and the Prince of Wales March 10th of the same year.] The Prince told us that he had never forgotten his disappointment on learning that General Tom Thumb had visited his royal mother, Queen Victoria, once when he, the Prince, had gone to bed. That was the General's first visit to the palace, and though he went several times afterward and saw the royal children, the Prince said his boyish disappointment over that first visit had never been wholly appeased.[22] The Duke of Cambridge was present, and he joined in the general laugh at the lugubrious face His Royal Highness assumed when he spoke of it. "You were not called General then," said the Prince. "No," replied my husband, "Her Majesty, Queen Victoria, gave me that title and I am as proud of that as I am of my American citizenship."

We also accepted an invitation to dine with the Reve[re]nd John Newman, since Cardinal Newman.

In December 1864 we left London for Paris, and my good fortune in never being seasick enabled me to enjoy every moment of our trip across the Channel. The General spoke French readily, but as none of the rest of us did—indeed, I'm such a rampant American

[that] I was never willing to acquire any other than my native language—our intercourse with the people we met was necessarily limited. At Paris we met many, I may say most, of the nobility. France was not a republic then, and after being summoned before the Emperor and Court, our success was assured. The beautiful Eugenie was one to be always remembered, and the Prince Imperial was a manly handsome boy apparently about nine years old. It seems pitiful somehow that he should have to die fighting in [an] English war.[23]

It has been whispered in Europe that there was a mutual attachment between the Prince Imperial and one of Victoria's daughters, but that the royal English mother forbade a marriage. One can't help wondering what changes that marriage might have made in history, and also drawing most comforting conclusions as to the freedom of choice in wedlock that exists among common people. Speaking of that reminds me that when recently in England, I heard it commonly spoken of that the devoted Beatrice, Victoria's youngest daughter, whom all the world honors for her devoted care during the closing years of her royal mother's life, had offers of marriage which promised much happiness, but the Queen forbade the consideration of any of them.

Notwithstanding the drawback of our ignorance of the language, we hoped to accomplish a good deal of sight-seeing, and did visit the tomb of Napoleon I at the Hôtel des Invalides, but the crowds that followed us made it so unpleasant getting about, we gave up trying.

I make a digression right here to say that my knowledge of embroidery did me good service and the General as well. When we were staying at any one place for a length of time, the confinement would have been irksome but for some employment with which to fill the hours. Naturally, we could not enjoy going out, to be followed, jostled and stared at by street crowds, so we began large pieces of embroidery. The General was particularly fond of it. He was naturally industrious and found it hard to sit idle in our rooms, and he made several pieces which together with my own were used in making the furniture of the home which he afterward built at Middleboro, Massachusetts. These were not "little" chairs etc. to accommodate ourselves, but of ordinary size to be used when we entertained our friends. One woman who called just out of curiosity,

77

after being received in a room much larger than her own at home, had the peculiar manners to say, "I'm disgusted to find your house not only as big as anybody's, but bigger than most folkses [*sic*]." The woman didn't seem to consider that if our house had been what she expected, she couldn't have come inside, and that the very maid who admitted her needed as much space as ordinary people.

Returning to London, we leased the house at No. 7 Bennett Street, leading from St. James' Street and next to the mansion belonging to the Marquis of Salisbury. We opened our levees in St. James' Hall, Piccadilly, and during our long stay there the hall was thronged early and late with nobility, gentry and all classes of citizens. Lord Ward, Earl of Derby, visited us frequently, and we came to look on him as a personal friend. Jenny Lind (Mme. Goldsmith) often attended our levees, bringing her children with her. We felt particularly drawn to her, not only for her gracious friendliness but also for her friendship for Mr. Barnum and her familiarity with America.[24] She spoke with such warm regard of her American friends and evinced such sympathetic enthusiasm when mention was made of our home country that our hearts warmed toward her as "own folks." We felt that those people in New York and Providence who paid two hundred and six hundred dollars for a ticket to hear her sing got their money's worth, but it was worth twice that to know her personally. In point of fact, when John N. Genin of New York paid two hundred and twenty-five dollars for the first ticket to Jenny Lind's concert, it was heralded all over the country; but when Ossian E. Dodge of Boston and M. A. Root of Philadelphia gave six hundred and twenty-five each, and Col. W. C. Ross of Providence six hundred and fifty, the public had become satisfied it was worth it and made no fuss over it.[25]

On June 25th, 1865, we were summoned to appear before Her Majesty Queen Victoria and the Royal Family at Windsor Castle. We gave an entertainment in the "Rubens Room." Princess Helena, Princess Louise, Princess Beatrice, Prince Leopold and a number of lords and ladies in waiting were present. At the conclusion of our performance the Queen signed for [the] General and me to approach her. She gently took my hand and, placing it upon her palm, looked at it with a smile and remarked, "It is smaller than an infant's." Then she questioned me about my home, my parents and my family,

78

frequently patting my hand as she talked. "I saw your husband many years ago," said she. "His name is quite a household word with us." She then reminded the General of the incident of his attacking her King Charles spaniel. The Princesses gathered around us and one of them exclaimed, "Oh, look at her dear little feet." I confess that, used as I was to comments on my personal appearance, I could feel the blushes covering my face.

The Duchess of Argyle took Minnie on her lap, laughingly persisting that "so tiny a mite was not too old to sit in lap," and all present gathered around us, our size breaking down all barriers of ettiquette [*sic*] and making us for the nonce "as good as anybody," as Minnie said. [The] Commodore added that if "a cat may look at a queen," surely free-born American citizens might do as much. Little did I then realize that I should live to see these royal boys and girls on many of the thrones of Europe.

There comes a tinge of sadness with these recollections of the past, but one of the warmest and pleasantest memories of my life is the memory of Queen Victoria as I saw her in the midst of her family. All the world admired her as a queen; those who met her personally revered and loved her as a woman. For Edward VII I can only ask, recalling the promise of his youth as I saw him that day, that he may prove her worthy successor.

After Her Majesty closed the interview, we were shown about the palace, a privilege we appreciated, as usually when the family is occupying it, strangers are excluded. Upon our return in the evening to St. James' Hall, the auditorium was crowded and we were received with cheers, as it was known we had just appeared before the Queen.

This repetition of my movements, receptions etc. must become monotonous to my readers, and I will hereafter devote more space to the description of what I saw of interest. Our party *not* being "personally conducted," we no doubt had better opportunities than most tourists of being shown objects and localities from the fact that we were, if I may use the term, "curiosities" ourselves; and the knowledge, widespread, that we had been favored by royalty appeared to act as an "open sesame" everywhere, and all were anxious to please and interest us. Finding in me an eager inquirer into the nature and history of all that was exhibited to us flattered and made

79

them more eager to open and show the contents of their choicest treasure houses. The very nature of our tour took us into towns and localities rich in historic relics which tourists rarely if ever visited and frequently never heard of.

[*Unfortunately for modern readers—who presumably no longer are the untraveled bumpkins their ancestors were—Lavinia makes good on the above promise and for the remainder of this and much of the five succeeding chapters devotes herself almost exclusively to detailing the history and architectural beauties of St. Paul's Cathedral and other venerable structures. The editor has felt free to delete all these passages, merely providing brief summaries in their stead, while faithfully preserving all those with direct relevance to Lavinia and her party. The remainder of the present chapter is taken up with a description of St. Paul's and its history.*]

Chapter 7

WESTMINSTER ABBEY, WITHIN WHOSE VENERABLE WALLS RE-
POSE THE REMAINS OF 13 ENGLISH SOVEREIGNS AND 14
QUEENS, REIGNING SOVEREIGNS OR THE CONSORTS OF KINGS,
COVERING A PERIOD OF 1,200 YEARS.

[*In this brief chapter Lavinia reports on what she learned and saw at Westminster Abbey, not omitting to mention the final resting place of Thomas Parr—a great "curiosity" in his own day—who died in 1635 at the reputed age of 152.* In my own family, *she adds*, my mother's cousin, Mrs. Rhoda Churchill of Middleboro, Massachusetts, has recently died at the age of one hundred and four.]

Chapter 8

THE TOWER OF LONDON, AS A FORTRESS, A PALACE AND A STATE PRISON. THE CROWNS, SCEPTERS AND REGALIA OF ENGLAND. THE TOWER AN EDUCATOR IN ENGLISH HISTORY.

[*Here Lavinia describes everything to be seen at the Tower of London, an obvious source of fascination to her, since she made many visits there. On one of these occasions, she writes,* I saw the block on which Lady Grey and others were executed and placed my fingers in the indentation made by the axe—such privilege (?) is seldom allowed.]

Chapter 9

FREQUENT VISITS TO ST. JAMES' PALACE. MRS. BRETTELL
WHO HELD THE MASTER KEY OF THE PALACE. AN INVITATION
TO TEA, THE GUEST REMAINING FOR 23 YEARS. A VISIT TO
HAMPTON COURT. DIFFERENT SOVEREIGNS WHO USED IT AS A
PALACE. A VERY OLD GRAPEVINE.

WHILE WE REMAINED in Great Britain all of our bills, programmes
etc. were headed with an impress of the Royal Coat of Arms, a
privilege only permitted to those who had been favored by Her
Majesty. A printer named Brettell did all of our work at his establishment.[26] He lived with his family, consisting of his wife, daughter
and two grandchildren. worthy young ladies, in apartments within
the walls of St. James' Palace. It is virtually the "Royal Palace." All
contracts of marriage of the reigning family and important state
papers are dated and signed within its wall[s]. Since the death of the
Prince Consort, the Queen seldom visits it except on important
occasions or when attending divine service or a funeral service in
[the] Royal Chapel. Mr. Brettell's privilege to occupy apartments
there was founded on the granting by King George IV to Mrs.
Brettell, at the age of 19, the important and responsible position of
custodian of the palace, with the sole right of holding the master key.

As no male was allowed to sleep within its walls, this matter was conveniently arranged by giving Mr. Brettell the nominal appointment of night watchman within. He faithfully performed his duty every night by going to bed and sleeping soundly. It was Mrs. Brettell's duty to receive the Queen or any member of the Royal Family when they entered the palace for state business or to attend service in the chapel; also to superintend the rooms, having them in order, particularly the throne room, preparatory to a "drawing room" being held; and also to nightly make a tour of the building and lock or secure every door of ingress or egress before retiring. She carried the keys to the wine vaults with permission to use such wines as she desired for her own table. She always carried the keys attached to her waist and at night placed them under her pillow. Remembering the size of the keys of those days, it certainly was no sinecure to lug around a "bunch" of them all day and have them under the pillow at night. One can readily fancy that with those under the pillow the poor woman's head might have lain as "uneasy" as the proverb says does that which "wears a crown." She had known Mr. Stratton ever since his first visit to England in 1844 and naturally was very desirous to see me, his wife. As she could not leave the palace, we accepted her invitation to call. She was then 83 years of age and a perfect picture of an old English dame. She insisted on our visiting her [as] often as possible, and scarcely a week passed that we did not dine or sup there with her and her family. It was amusing to observe the great care with which she carried the wine from the vaults to decant it for our dinner, a duty she always performed herself. She glided along as if the slightest jar would disturb any sediment and poured the contents of the bottles into the decanters carefully and gently, always mentioning the age of the wine. The vaults were stocked each year with the vintages of that particular year. They contained wines sixty, seventy and eighty years old.

There was but one other resident in the palace; she was a spinster named Miss Norton, a very old acquaintance of Mrs. Brettell's. She had no known relative living. One afternoon she called to take tea with Mrs. B. She remained rather late and Mrs. B. told her she had better remain all night, which she did, occupying an apartment at the other end of the palace. The next day she took breakfast, dinner and tea and retired at night without making any reference to her departure, and so continued day after day for twenty-three years. Mrs. B., pitying her lonely condition, did not suggest her going but permitted her to remain. They weren't crowded even then. Whenever any visitor called on Mrs. B. and Miss Norton entered a stranger to them, Mrs. B., with a merry twinkle in her eye, would introduce her thus: "This is Miss Norton, an old friend of mine who just dropped in to take tea with me—twenty-three years ago."

Mrs. Brettell being ill one day, sent her daughter to receive Her Majesty and the Prince of Wales, who had unexpectedly visited the palace. As it was the first time the daughter had performed the office, she was extremely nervous and, in her attempt to make a low sweeping courtesy, caught her foot in her dress and to her great mortification sat down upon the floor with greater emphasis than grace. The situation was so ludicrous that the Queen hid her smiles behind her handkerchief, while the Prince hastily lifted the frightened woman to her feet with a kind inquiry as to whether she was injured.

I once asked Mrs. Brettell if she ever felt timid or frightened while going through the palace late at night. She replied, "I never felt timid but once, and that was when the remains of his late Majesty, King William IV, lay in state in the throne room. I loved him dearly; he was a good, kind, handsome man, so gracious to me. When I entered the room with the dim lights burning, having to cross to reach the other end of the palace, I stopped and, looking towards the body, it seemed as if a sudden fear took possession of me. It appeared to me as if he had partly arisen and was looking at me with the same kind look with which he always greeted me. For a few moments my limbs trembled beneath me. After a time, with a great effort I overcame the fear partly and hastily ran across the apartment close beside the body, turning my head away as I passed. Having fulfilled my duties, courage came to me again, and when I returned I stopped and looked upon his dear face, then retired and locked the door."

Kind dear old Mrs. Brettell! The last time I saw and parted from her was during my second visit to England in 1873. She was then 90 years old. She was lying upon her bed in her last illness, with characteristic faithfulness still holding in her hand the old keys. During her illness the daughter attended to the official duties, but immediately after using the keys placed them again in her mother's hand.

I devoted several days to visiting Hampton Court. The notes I took of what I saw in palaces and castles have served to recal[l] the sights to my mind; and they have greatly served me now while writing this book.

[*The remainder of the chapter is a description of Hampton Court, where Lavinia marveled at the great grapevine and presumably delighted in getting lost in the maze.*]

Chapter 10

THE CITY OF CHESTER, THE ONLY WALLED CITY IN GREAT
BRITAIN. ROMAN REMAINS. GOD'S PROVIDENCE HOUSE.
BOW BRIDGE. STRANGE PROPHECY REGARDING THE DEATH OF
KING RICHARD III.

AFTER REMAINING IN LONDON over a year, we started on a tour
through the country, giving entertainments in all of the principal
cities and towns in the kingdom. It would be impossible to follow in
detail our route and describe all I saw in ancient towns, palaces and
castles. I will, however, transcribe a few as my memory serves,
while I glance over my unarranged notes—not having placed them
in continuity.

[*The rest of this brief chapter, consisting of barely two leaves, is concerned
with the history and sights of Chester and a visit to Shakespeare's birthplace.*]

Chapter 11

[*In revising her manuscript Lavinia discarded the original first leaf of this chapter, and with it the "contents" which appear at the heads of the other chapters in their first-draft state. Although the process of revision also seems to have unintentionally obliterated the division between this and the following chapter, it would appear that the present one was devoted solely to Coventry, where the party arrived during the "Great Fair" and Lavinia immersed herself in the history of Lady Godiva and Peeping Tom. During the Fair she witnessed the representative of Lady Godiva riding in the procession and was pleased to observe that she was* modest in her bearing *and wore a* decorous costume in lieu of the former imitation of nudity.]

[Chapter 12]

[*There is no explicit indication of a twelfth chapter in the manuscript as it presently stands. Again, the process of revision seems to have led to this oversight.*]

We visited most of the cities and towns of England, Scotland, Wales and Ireland (208 in number), with but little incident to mark either.[27] But I recall one at Peterboro. A glossy plausible stranger called to show us some diamonds. The General was delighted with them and very pleased with the urbane dealer, who in the blandest manner suggested that he leave the diamonds, let me wear them at our entertainment that night and see how I liked them, and he, the owner, would call in the morning. To all of which Mr. Stratton most cordially consented. I wouldn't like to say that I was any less honest than my husband, but women do seem to have a sort of sixth sense sometimes and I firmly refused. After the man was gone, Mr. Stratton asked my reason for so doing. "Because," I said, "it's not reasonable to suppose that a perfect stranger would leave diamonds with us, and I believe he expected to steal them during the night, make us pay for them in the morning and then walk off in possession of the money and the diamonds both." Man-like, the General didn't

89

confess to a conversion to my opinion, but giving a long whistle, he walked out and closed the door.

While at Maidstone I received calls from Lady Franklin, whose husband was lost in his search for the North Pole, and from Queen Emma of the Sandwich Islands. I don't recall much of the personal appearance of either of them, but my irreverent husband said when he was presented to Lady Franklin, he could think of nothing but the New Orleans newsboy who called, in order to "work off" his papers, "Sir John Franklin found!" Some doubting bystander asked, "What was Sir John doing when they found him?" "Sitting on the North Pole hatching snowballs," was the prompt reply.

A comical episode in Glasgow was a source of merriment to our whole party for many days after. As we were driving to the hall one afternoon, we met a funeral. The coffin was placed in the bottom of a peculiar vehicle, and the mourners (presumably) sat on either side facing each other, and if not resting their feet on the coffin must have had some difficulty in avoiding it. Looking at them with all the sympathy such an occasion is likely to command, we observed the lugubrious expression of their faces change suddenly as they caught sight of our equipage.[28] From simple surprise it grew to astonished wonderment, and our surprise was no less when, deserting the coffin, they sprang to the roadway and eagerly followed our carriage till they had seen us leave it and enter the hall. Doubtless the corpse waited their return with equanimity, but we never learned whether that burial was finished up on time. For many days afterward any allusion among us to a funeral would evoke shouts of unseemly laughter.

In Ireland we were entertained most delightfully by members of the nobility who reside in Dublin, and our levees in Rotunda Hall were crowded. We went to Phoenix Park, little dreaming of the terrible associations it has later acquired.[29] We took rides in a "jaunting car," on one of which, being assured it was a necessary proceedure [sic], we stopped at a mud hut built in the bank for a "dhrop of the cratur," which was served to us by a rosy-faced old woman in petticoat and short gown and finished off above with a broad frilled cap. That was before the days of the W.C.T.U. [Women's Christian Temperance Union], and the old woman and the mud hut were a part of the regular show to which tourists were treated. The whiskey was a necessary "cue." On a later visit to Ireland with Mr.

Stratton only, we visited Blarney Castle and my husband insisted on being lowered by his feet till he was able to kiss the Blarney Stone, though I stoutly maintained the ceremony was quite superfluous for him. I gazed at the soles of his boots in mortal terror and was thankful his weight was no greater. The probable result of a heavier man's attempt is appalling, though as a friend suggested, any man who'd try it needn't fear having his brains dashed out, as a paucity of the article would be evidenced by the attempt. I took care that the General didn't hear her remark.

We went the length and breadth of the island, repeating pleasant experiences at every turn. We were there at Christmas, but gave no levee that day as the people look upon it as a holy day. Remembering what it commemorates, there seems every reason to agree with them.

After my marriage to the Count I again visited Ireland in 1887, and at that time we received a call from Prince Edward of Saxe Wiemer [sic]. He was accompanied by his lovely wife, who proposed to send her carriage for us next day. The sudden illness of her mother prevented [this], and she sent a note of regret, acquainting us with the cause. Her mother died before our departure and we did not see Her Highness again. A friend in Belfast sent me some shamrock while I was at Warrenton, England. Hoping to keep it fresh enough to show its nationality, I secured a large potatoe, scooped it out, and enclosing the shamrock sent it home to the United States. There the potatoe and shamrock both were carefully and prayerfully planted. The shamrock was homesick and pined away, but the potatoe, remembering its nativity, took vigorous root and grew merrily, developing sundry small tubers which evidently intended to be potatoes and do credit to a free soil. But a curious biped yclept John, anxious to "see what was at the bottom," as he said, pulled them up to investigate. His efforts to replant them were not successful. He had found out what was down there, and his mother thinks he found out more than that. He himself is reticent on the subject.

[*The above digressions, by Lavinia's own admission, have led to some momentary confusion in the chronology of her narrative, and she now compounds the confusion by referring to the same troupe's tour round the world and return to America from Britain several years later. After apparently regaining her bearings, she concludes the chapter with the statement that the repatriated party,* after resting a while in Middleboro, Massachusetts, began a second tour of the United States and Canada the following November.]

Chapter 13[30]

THE CIVIL WAR HAVING PREVENTED US from going to the extreme South previously, our party took occasion now to visit all of the southern states, going as far to the southwest as San Antonio, Texas, eighty miles from Austin, which distance we drove (there being then no [rail]way) in fourteen hours, including the fording of two [streams?] or rather what they down there call "creeks," and in Louisiana a "bayou." The funny thing about these creeks is that they lie at the bottom of a sort of ditch, and to cross one you have to go down a steep slope first, get across the muddy creek as best you can and then climb up again. One of our party said, "In this country the hills are scooped out instead of built up." We started down the steep bank and held on for dear life to straps, seats or anything we could grasp to escape pitching forward on the struggling mules, who however seemed to understand their business and made no protest when the wagon pushed on them, but slipped and slid down to the water's edge and splashed in. Now let it be remembered that the streams in that part of the country are not clear and transparent as they are here, but being sluggish they hold in solution the clay and are therefore the color of whatever soil they run through—if they can be said to "run." Minnie said she'd heard of running streams, but these only walked. It is this peculiarity of color which has often given them their names, such as "Red River," "White River," "Yellowstone" etc. This particular stream was about the color of coffee with milk in it—and a good deal thicker than I like my coffee—[and] therefore gave no opportunity for us to guess what might be beneath the surface. So we were in terror of holes or rocks, forgetting for the moment that rocks are an unknown quantity in that section of the country. Once over the stream, the mules struggled up the slippery bank on the other side; and this was even more disconcerting than the pitching down, for one doesn't like to contemplate the possibility of team and all going backwards into the water, or if the team doesn't *you* may, and the prospect of a plunge into *that* water reminded me of an old man at home who used to say, "I can stand bein' run over, but I don't want ter be run over by a swill cart." Arrived at the second stream the process must be repeated, but the gentlemen of the party got out, declaring they'd find some means of getting over without the aid of the mules. A brown log lay just at the edge of the water, somewhat muddy but offering a chance, it seemed, if it should prove long enough, for them to make an impromptu if somewhat precarious bridge. So our pianist procured a sort of lever and proceeded to pry it round. I watched him with a good deal of interest, for I thought if he succeeded I'd follow his lead, for my nerves hadn't quite forgotten the experience of a few hours before at the other stream. Fixing his lever as firmly as the soft mud would allow, he began prying the log around. It moved slightly with his first effort, and calling for assistance, he readjusted his lever and pried again. This started it, and with a sudden hitch that sprawled the men in the mud a "fourteen-foot" alligator distended astonished jaws and plunged into the water.

You may have seen scared men! So have I! The alligator swam off downstream, and as I remember nobody invited him back. The sudden splash of the "'gator" and the alarmed shouts of the men startled the mules, and the excited driver hurried them across and up the opposite bank without waiting for the gentlemen to climb aboard, and when on the other side we were confronted with the problem of getting the party together again. At last the driver, who was a native, shouted, "Say, you all'll hev to coon it over on that tree." I had never heard the expression "coon it," but as I looked at the tree he pointed out, which had fallen across the stream some distance above, I comprehended. The stranded men scrambled toward the tree. Some of the most venturesome walked awkwardly part of the way, but soon fell on their knees and with the rest "cooned it" as directed.

San Antonio is a charming city, and the two rivers running through it are veritable rivers and add greatly to its beauty as well as making it quite unlike other places. A part of the city is still almost entirely Mexican, and we were a little chagrined to find the daily paper we bought printed in Spanish. Our audiences were mixed, but they seemed to think their eyes could comprehend what their ears might fail of. Even so soon after the war when, remembering the generous self-sacrifice of those people, one might imagine there would be little money for sight-seeing, our trip netted us about one thousand dollars a week.

One more episode of that trip I will give, because the days when it was possible have gone by forever. It was at Opelika, Tennessee. We went to a hotel which was not an unusual specimen at that time. The lower floor was largely occupied by one room with a huge open fireplace at one end. The stairs were of rough boards not unlike those that carpenters use before putting up the final ones. Our rooms were on the second floor, and when we discovered that the flight of steps which led to the third floor was only a ladder, we congratulated ourselves on that fact. The place seemed so desolate that we were glad to gather in one room. To add to our nervousness, someone had discovered, chalked roughly on a door, the figures "11:35," and in some occult way the idea had spread among us that this meant the hour when the man within was to die at the hands of the Ku Klux [Klan]. Poor Commodore was suffering from an attack of quinsy, and we were so anxious about him that we had less thought of danger from any other source. Suddenly we were startled by the report of two pistols fired in quick succession. Mrs. Bleeker sprang up and rushed toward the door, despite the terrified entreaties of the group about the table. "But," she said, "I want to know where my husband is." At this juncture Mr. Bleeker entered, deathly pale but calm and quiet, and said, "Get on your wraps, the 'bus for the station is at the door." Quickly as possible we complied, and wrapping the Commodore in a blanket, Mr. Bleeker took him in his arms and carried him downstairs. We followed, only to see the 'bus rapidly disappearing in the direction of the station, bearing within its unfilled interior the other members of our party. Seeing our distress, the landlord with the utmost kindness assured us that the 'bus would soon return, and if it didn't we could stay all night at his hotel and be taken to an early train in the morning. The prospect of staying there all night was not reassuring, and there was a strained look in Mr. Bleeker's face, when he persisted in going, which we didn't understand till later. Arrived at the station, Commodore was made as comfortable as circumstances permitted, and then we composed ourselves to wait for a train two hours late. To enliven the waiting, certain natives whose skillfully ejected saliva seemed likely to extinguish the open fire began giving particulars of sundry incidents which at that time were fresh in everybody's mind. One was of an engineer who had been taken from his engine and tarred and feathered. Another obnoxious man had been silently hung on a neighboring tree. One woman had been taken from her bed and whipped, then tied to a tree to await possible rescue.

These things seemed to strike no one as out of the common, but to us they seemed a trifle unusual to say the least, and we were in a fever of anxiety lest the train should not arrive before some of these pleasant gentlemen should conceive the idea that we might be considered suitable ornaments for telegraph poles. Once safe in Nashville, Mr. Bleeker told us that while passing through the room below us at the hotel he had been accosted by two men who were sitting by the fire, both of whom appeared to be drunk. They cordially urged him to be seated between them, and when he declined pressed him to take a drink. This he too declined as gently and politely as possible, saying he must join the ladies. Coming immediately upstairs, before entering the room where we were he stepped out on the "gallery," only to see the two supposably [sic] drunken men standing outside as erect and firmly as himself. At the instant he appeared one of them raised a pistol and fired at him. At the first motion, Mr. B. had dodged behind a post and remained there till the report of the second pistol assured him that for the moment the pistols were empty. Then he came to us and began preparations for our immediate departure. "Well," said our pianist, "those of us who could scurried into that first 'bus, for we had seen enough to convince us it wasn't wise to stand upon the order of our going, but to get out of town as quickly as possible was the best thing we could do. What we saw on the road deepened this conviction, but we were in an agony of apprehension concerning the rest of you, till we saw you enter the station. And now I'm very glad you weren't in the first 'bus to see what we saw." Asked to explain, he said that as they drove toward the station "there appeared suddenly and silently a line of ghostly figures on horseback. Each man was enveloped in a white overdress of some sort on which was rudely depicted the outlines of a skeleton. Head and face were covered by a quaint white cap with erect ears on top, which might have been intended for horns, and two holes cut to allow vision. The horses were also covered with white so as to effectually conceal their bodies, and with hoods and eye holes to add grotesqueness to their heads. Our own horses shied and snorted with terror, but not a head in that ghastly line turned toward us. Silent and statuesque, the uncanny file moved on with no sound save the muffled thud of the horses' feet in the dust, giving no clue to its destination or from whence it came. Even as it was passing, another figure rode out from behind a shanty where it had been concealed and wheeled into line without a word of welcome or command. In Indian file they kept on their way, and the onlookers felt, as it was intended they should, the oppression of the silence and mystery."

I've been told that the Ku Klux as originally formed was quite largely composed of gentleman's [*sic*] sons, but either other elements had crept in or else vagabonds and thieves had borrowed their uniforms and were taking advantage of the local excitement to commit murder and robbery. There seemed no room for doubt that they intended to rob us, committing any murder that might be necessary to accomplish their object.

In May 1869 Mr. Barnum wrote to Mr. Bleeker the following letter[31]:

Lindencroft, May 10th, 1869

My dear Bleeker:

An idea has occurred to me in which I can see a "Golden Gate" opening for the Gen. Tom Thumb Co. What do you think of a "Tour around the World," including a visit to Australia? The new Pacific Railroad will be finished in a few weeks; you will then be enabled to cross the American Continent to California, thence by steam to Japan, China, British India etc. I declare, in anticipation, I already envy you the pleasures and opportunities which such a trip will afford.

For the next three days I shall study all the maps I can lay my hands upon and, in imagination, mark you crossing the briny deep to those far-off countries. And as for *gold*! tell the General that in Australia alone (don't fail to go to Australia) he will be sure to make more money than a horse can draw.

It will require great care, judgement, experience and energy, all of which faculties you possess, to carry such an enterprise to a successful termination.

Talk it over with the "little people." I name you Generalissimo of the invading force in their grand march, and hope you will return with spoils from all nations of the globe.

Decide quickly. If you consent to undertake the journey, prepare to start next month. Love to all,

Truly yours,
P. T. Barnum

Mr. Bleeker laid this letter before us, and through his persuasion we consented. We hastened our return to New York that we might prepare for our long journey. Taking a vacation of two weeks to replenish our wardrobes, visit our friends to bid them farewell and to make provision for our long absence, we were at the conclusion of that time ready to start.

On the morning of June 21st, 1869, the Gen. Tom Thumb Company left the City of New York for a "three years' tour around the world." The following members composed the troupe:

Sylvester Bleeker	Director and Manager
Mrs. S. Bleeker	
B. S. Kellogg	Treasurer
Edmund Davis	Agent

GEN. TOM THUMB AND WIFE
COMMODORE NUTT
MISS MINNIE WARREN

G. H. Richardson	Pianist	F. G. Nobbs	Doorkeeper
C. E. Keeler	Genl. Assist't	Rod[n]ia Nutt, Jr.[32]	Coachman
	G. Cooper, Groom		

A pair of diminutive ponies and miniature carriage completed the retinue. If the weather suggested a good or ill omen, it was a gloomy prospect, for it rained in torrents; besides, our company numbered thirteen—which was a source of worry to some of our friends who had come to see us off and had discovered the fact. But Mr. Bleeker allayed their fears by assuring them that the company was comprised of 15 members, the ponies being counted as two persons as he always paid their fares on the railroad at that rate. With the strictest injunctions from our friends to write often, to be careful of our health and not to forget to bring something from "those foreign countries," we departed.

Let it be remembered that a trip around the world then was quite a different thing from what it is now in these days of "Raymondies" and "Cookies," with planned stereotyped routes and hotel rooms engaged ahead, agents to take you when and where *they* list, and whirl you by train and trolley past all the places where you want to go and land you by night in darkness in the especial places you don't want to see.

Notwithstanding torrents of rain on the day we started and our ominous number, we went off in high glee on a trip which proved healthful, pleasant and profitable. I think our manager reported eighty thousand dollars to Mr. Barnum. Our planned route involved an average travel of one hundred and ten miles and the giving two entertainments each day. This is sufficient answer to the question as to whether we had mature bodies, whatever may be thought of our brains. Our journey over the Union Pacific Railway in which the last spike had just been driven included one space of twenty-six hours continuous travel.

Before leaving civilization, so to speak, kind friends had entertained us with stories of attacks on trains by Indians, which were not exactly suited to act as opiates, the first night at least. We saw a good many of these redskins stalking about from time to time, and our fancies and fears grew perceptably [*sic*] as the train hastened on. Many of the passengers armed themselves. We left Omaha Sunday, July 11th, at 8 A.M. As we sped along, several of the passengers, as if to exhibit to others how well they could handle their rifles, would occasionally fire them out of the windows. Immediately back of us was seated a portly gentleman who was evidently getting nervous. He touched Mr. Bleeker on the shoulder and said, "Do you think there is any danger?" "From what?" inquired Mr. B. "Indians," said he. "I see that a number of the passengers are armed in anticipation, and I understand that each train carries arms and ammunition sufficient and ready to supply every man, woman and child on board. Now I never fired a gun in all my life. What should I do? Are those men practising in case of attack or merely firing their guns to let the savages know, if any are lurking in ambush near, that we are prepared?" "There's not a tree or bush large enough to conceal a foe for miles around," said Mr. B.

At that moment some person in sport shouted "Indians!" Passengers' heads were quickly thrust out of the windows; some rushed for the doors. Our fat friend with a groan sprang to his feet, looked around with horror depicted in his countenance and made a dive beneath the seat. The space being narrow, he succeeded only in getting his head and shoulders hidden, and there he stuck. When the false alarm was made apparent, all returned laughing to their seats, but it was with great difficulty that our plethoric gentleman was extricated from his uncomfortable position.

We arrived at Cheyenne at 8 A.M. the following day. Between Valley and Fremont, forty-six miles from Omaha, we first came in sight of the Platte River and continued in view of it for three hundred miles. We saw very many antelopes during our journey and couldn't fail to admire their graceful beauty. They paid little attention to us, however, but the myriads of prairie dogs interested us greatly. Their comical way of sitting erect and staring at our train, then with a flourish of heels and tails disappearing into the earth, excited screams of laughter from each and all.

This road is now so much travelled, the scenery along its line has been so often described and has changed so materially, [that] it would be superfluous for me to attempt an idea of it. Most of the towns which are now flourishing places were merely canvas stations with an occasional adobe house used as a base of supplies for the men building the road. Liquor and gambling were the chief features of these wild places.

Cheyenne then had a population of 4,000 inhabitants. Upon alighting from the cars, we were met and warmly greeted by Mr. E. C. Z. Judson (Ned Buntline), who did everything in his power to make us comfortable.[33] We exhibited in the "Theatre," a tumble-down rickety old barn with rough boards for seats, contrasting most comically with some we had left behind. However, it was filled to overflowing at each performance. The most prominent features of the city, as it was called, were barrooms and gambling houses. Returning from the theatre to the hotel, a distance of 300 yards, we counted out of curiosity the number of barrooms we passed, and they numbered 37, all brilliantly lighted by kerosene while an equally inflammable liquid was being imbibed by their denizens, who in full view rattled their gambling "layouts," I think they term them.

We next proceeded to Laramie and from thence to Ogden, the first town of note in Utah on the Pacific road, 1032 miles from Omaha. That there was a stringent controlling power was evidenced in its clean streets and good dwellings. It then had a population of 2,000 inhabitants. A Mormon bishop and mayor held the governmental reins. They granted the use of their tabernacle for our entertainment, reserving however the use of two rows of seats, capable of accommodating 50 persons, for their families. It was here that I first saw the effect of practical polygamy. The bishop, while waiting for the arrival of his family, informed Mr. Bleeker that he was a native of New Hampshire and had joined the Mormons 30 years before. Looking at his watch, he said that as it was near the hour for us to commence our entertainment he would go and notify his brother. He departed and in a few moments returned, followed by his brother, seven adult females and 42 children varying in ages from 3 to 14 years; then came 3 females and 22 children, the bishop saying to Mr. Bleeker as they passed, "My family."

During our entertainment Mr. Bleeker always invited a dozen children from 3 to 10 years of age to come upon the stage and compare their height with Miss Minnie's diminutive stature. Upon this occasion Bishop West, standing in the aisle at the end of the seat containing his family, immediately passed the requisite number to the platform. Mr. B., having placed the smallest of them nearest to Minnie, then, in order that he might not be suspected of misrepresenting the children's age[s], requested the parents to give it. Pointing to the first child, a light curly haired little fellow, Mr. B. inquired, "What is this child's age?" "Four years," replied the bishop. "Yours?" said Mr. B. He nodded. "And this one?" said Mr. B., pointing to a black-eyed little girl. "Four years," again replied the bishop, with rising color. "Yours?" said Mr. B. Again he nodded.

101

"And the age of this child?" said Mr. B., touching a sturdy little one. "Four," exclaimed the bishop, the blood mantling to his forehead. "Yours?" inquired Mr. B. He bowed. "And this?" questioned Mr. B., laying his hand upon the head of a pale-faced interesting little boy. "Four," replied the bishop, his face a crimson. "Yours?" again inquired Mr. B. "All of them," replied the bishop faintly. For the moment I felt so indignant that I could not help calling to Mr. Bleeker from the side where I stood, "Ask no more; it is disgraceful." I do not know what more I might have said, but Mr. Bleeker motioned me to be silent.

The landlord of the hotel where we staid had ten wives, and the General said he hoped the "pin money" wouldn't bankrupt him, a remark I silently resented. When we paid our bill we *concluded it wouldn't!*

The construction of the railway from Ogden to Salt Lake City had not then been commenced. Wells, Fargo & Co.'s line of stages started from the Uinta for Salt Lake City only on certain days, and as there were two small towns lying upon the direct road which would serve as stopping places to break the fatigue of the journey, an arrangement was made with a resident of Salt Lake City to meet us at Ogden early on the following Sunday morning to convey us to the city in two large comfortable vehicles. He arrived the evening before our intended departure. We had bargained for "comfortable vehicles," but evidently there is room for a difference of opinion in the matter, for our "comfortable vehicles" consisted of dead-axle box wagons, each drawn by two mules. Now the mule is not an exhilerating animal, and nowhere that I know, except in the frieze on the outside of the Pension Office at the nation's capitol [sic], has his virtues been immortalized in sculpture; but it is well to remember that the "army mule" plays an important part in our wars and that, conditions being supplied [sic], he "gets there." As there was no alternative, we submitted to the discomfort and started for Farmington. The road was rough, barren and rocky. About four miles from Ogden we mounted the level of a high plateau and from there we caught our first glimpse of the Great Salt Lake, looking magnificently blue in the distance as it lay calm and quiet, not a ripple nor a sign of life upon it. In Australia I saw the famed "Blue Lake" lying in the crater of an extinct volcano, but for brilliancy of color as it

102

gleamed in the sunlight, even that marvel of azure beauty cannot compare with Salt Lake.

Farmington then contained a population of 600—and not a Gentile in the town! We stopped with a Mormon who had two wives in the house. His first wife was over 60 years of age, his other wife 35 with 2 small children. The daughter by the first wife lived adjoining. She was married and had several children. We gave two entertainments and departed the next morning for Bountiful, our road lying beside the Great Lake. It was on this road for the first time we saw a noble specimen of the red man. I had seen numerous Indians before who did not exactly fill my Cooperized ideals. I had a fancy that a cake of Ivory Soap, a hairbrush and some perfumery might improve matters. This one was tall, splendidly proportioned and straight as an arrow, his skin of a clear copper color and his features finely chiseled; not a vestige of paint marred their expression. He was dressed in a deerskin hunting shirt, girded with a broad belt at the waist from which a hunting knife protruded; his leggings were fringed with hair and his mocassins were richly worked with wampum. Around his head he wore a scarlet band with three large eagle's feathers; in his hand he carried a rifle. His step was firm and elastic. As he crossed our path he did not deign a glance but, looking straight before him, stalked proudly by. His whole appearance was in such striking contrast with the filthy degenerate-looking beings we had seen that we gazed in admiration upon him as a true type of the pure American Indian before contact with the whites had reduced them to their present degraded level.

The next day, after appearing at North Cañon or Bountiful as it was called, we arrived at Salt Lake City. Mr. John Young called on us at the Townsend House and said that his father would be happy to receive the General and party. The next day being appointed for our visit, we went and were cordially received by Brigham Young, and a pleasant hour was spent in social converse. He told his son John to take us under his special care while we remained in the city and to be sure to take us out to "the farm." We visited "the farm" and were much entertained. It was 4 miles from the city. Several acres of it were devoted to the raising of the mulberry tree and the breeding of the silkworm. A large building had been erected, presided over by a Frenchman, in which we saw thousands of worms in the various stages of silk spinning. We were each presented with a cocoon. During our stay in the city Mr. John Young was very attentive. With him as guide, we saw everything worthy of note and probably some things that later and larger people may not have seen. We met not only Brigham Young, but Heber Kimball, Elder Woodruff and many others whose names meant little to us then but are now conspicuous in history.

On the morning of July 24th we were awakened at daybreak by the booming of cannon, the sharp report of pistols and the snapping of firecrackers. The General suggested that the Mormon calendar had got belated and we were having our Fourth of July over again. On investigation, we learned that this was the celebration of the twenty-second anniversary of the arrival of the pioneers at Salt Lake. The plans for the day included speeches, processions, military parades etc. The chief address was by Brigham Young. An original song was written by J. D. T. McAllister, who also figured as Chief Marshall of the procession. I append it, as it will give a clear idea of the sentiment as well as the poetry of the occasion.

[*The song, a paean celebrating Brigham Young and the blessed state of those under his inspired leadership, is reprinted in Bleeker's book.*]

Over ten thousand persons from the surrounding country had come in to witness the celebration. The procession was admirably conducted. The line of march leading past the Townsend House, the landlord kindly erected a platform in front of the hotel for our especial use and from which we witnessed it.[34] In the afternoon we attended the services at the Tabernacle.

From Salt Lake City we went to Corinne, lying upon the line of the Union Pacific Railway. Alighting from the cars, we waded in sand knee-deep to a large canvas building with the sign "Uinta Hotel" painted in huge letters across the front. Corinne was originally a camp, but being directly upon the road it became an excellent depot for the supply of Brigham City lying six miles back. I have before spoken of the canvas towns, the only wood used in the construction of the dwellings being a slight framework. During the building of the railroad, Corinne had a population of 10,000, but it was now reduced to 2,000. The rooms of the "Uinta Hotel," if rooms they could be called, were "all in a row." Two wooden partitions six feet high and three feet apart formed a hall extending the full length. At intervals of six feet an opening was cut and a rough door suspended. The rooms were divided off by hanging old army blankets, remnants of unbleached sheeting, pieces of old calico etc. These little divisions or rooms were six feet square. The bedsteads consisted of two narrow strips of wood four feet apart, supported on props twelve inches high, with narrow slats across, upon which a very thin mattress was placed, covered with one brown sheet and a dirty army blanket. Two boards were placed beside this bed for a flooring. Owing to the limited space I was compelled to disrobe upon the bed. The lavatory was at the end of the passageway, in an opening leading to an adjoining canvas house used as the dining room, and was supplied with two old tin pans placed upon a low shelf, one piece of hard yellow soap, a bucket of water with a tin dipper and one large "jack towel" for the accommodation of over 30 guests. I left my luxurious couch by daylight. We gave two entertainments in a canvas house used as a billiard room.

The next day two very respectable-looking vehicles were engaged to convey us to Brigham City. Upon the route we passed by an Indian camp and saw the squaws busily engaged cooking, dressing buffalo skins etc. A few of the brave warriors sat or lounged beside their wigwams lazily smoking. We found Brigham City to be a very pleasant cheerful place, possessing one wide main street upon which were located a dozen stores, a good hotel, post office and town hall. Elder Snow had a fine residence surrounded by a high wall. I was told by the citizens that he was very much more married than Brigham Young, the number of his wives exceeding that of the President. Perhaps that accounted for the wall!

Shortly after our arrival we observed an Indian making himself very free in the hotel while his squaw and her papoose squatted upon the ground outside. He was chief of the Ute tribe, encamped upon the plain we had passed on our road across. This chief had saved the life of the landlord's brother seventeen years before. His name interpreted was "Springing Panther"; the whites called him "Joseph." I thought then as I think now that the assumption of a right to re-name Indians, which is so common, is as derogatory to the dignity of the white man as of the Indian. We don't presume to address Mr. Wentworth Higgenbottem as "Jim Jones" because it is easier to speak, and this persistent "calling names" when addressing Indians lowers our standard of civility, though fortunately in his pride of race the Indian doesn't recognize the possibility of any loss of self-respect. With all his faults and filth, he has the advantage of us in some things. I asked the landlord to admit the squaw, but he said it would not be safe for she would steal anything she could lay hands upon; however, at length he consented and admitted her. Trailing behind her was a long rope, and when we called her attention to it, she gravely announced there was a pony at the other end of it. It being her duty to tether the pony, she didn't propose to neglect it for mere sight-seeing, so as she mounted the stairs she simply paid out the rope and left the pony grazing below. Feeling grateful that she had not thought it necessary to bring the pony up too, we entertained her to the best of our ability, the landlord acting as interpreter. She compared Minnie's size with her papoose and showed wonder and admiration. Finally she and her husband disappeared.

Shortly after supper we heard a terrible whooping and yelling and, looking out to discover the cause, saw 40 or 50 Indians mounted upon their ponies dashing down the street. Stopping in front of the hotel, they dismounted. The squaw had evidently told them about us. Joseph stood apart. Mr. Bleeker signified that if he would draw his warriors a few paces back from the building, he would allow us to appear at the window. Joseph ordered them back. When they saw us, they jabbered and gazed and nodded their heads to each other approvingly, holding their hands about a yard from the ground, signifying how small we were. Mr. Bleeker then presented each one separately with a gilt locket containing our photographs, of a kind we sold at the conclusion of our entertainment. They received them with great satisfaction. When the little carriage appeared to convey us to the hall, they surrounded it and accompanied us—a strange and fantastic bodyguard. They would have followed us into the hall, but Joseph said something to them, pointing to their encampment; they immediately dashed off whooping and yelling. The chief Joseph, however, entered and, stretching himself upon a large wood box standing beside the stove, remained until the close of the performance.[35]

Two days prior to our arrival in Brigham City the mutilated body of one of the same tribe had been found in the cañon, and the Indians, under the supposition that he had been killed by a white man, had declared that they would have the lives of three palefaces in compensation. This was rather startling intelligence for us, as we were compelled to return to Corinne at the end of the evening performance in Brigham City. Mr. Bleeker inquired of the landlord as to the fact, and he said there was no doubt that the redskin had been killed by one of his comrades after having drank and gambled together. The landlord appealed to two hunters for the truth of the story to show there would be no danger in our starting upon the journey. One of the hunters, however, said to Mr. B., "Them dirty skunks are treacherous as a razor. They know you are strangers and wouldn't be missed. I don't think there is much danger, for they don't want to make enemies of us, but I'd advise you to keep together on the road; you will look like a strong party. If you had 12 or 15 miles to go I wouldn't insure you; as it is, they would be afraid to use their rifles, for that would bring us down upon 'em, and they will hardly attack you with knives and hatchets. Go quietly and give them as wide a berth as possible." Mr. B. thanked him for his advice and at midnight had the vehicles ready for us to start. It had been a moonlit evening, but it became very cloudy and dark. As we passed within 500 yards of the village, all of us kept strict silence. Several dogs began to bark, and half a dozen dusky forms glided to and fro on the outskirts as if just aroused. A heavy rain set in which made it very uncomfortable, and we were glad to take shelter under the canvas roof of the Uinta Hotel.

From Corinne we proceeded west, visiting most of the towns. At Virginia City we performed in a fine opera house [*Piper's*] for 3 days; our receipts averaged $1,200 per day. Traveling by stage was perilous in consequence of the roads being beset by highwaymen. There were four gentlemanly appearing men we had observed regularly attending our performances. They intruded themselves upon Mr. Bleeker, insisting on his joining them in taking wine and in conversation, speaking of my elegant diamonds, the great amount of money we must carry with us judging from the business we were doing, etc. etc. After the afternoon performance the last day of our stay, they walked with Mr. B. to the hotel to take a parting drink. One of them casually remarked, "As you go to Reno tomorrow, you cannot give a matinee there as the stage does not leave here until 12 o'clock; but you will get there in time for the evening entertainment." Mr. B. acquiesced and said, "We must expect to lose many entertainments where communication between towns is restricted as to starting time." After a time they shook hands and parted. Soon as they were well out of sight, Mr. B. went to Wells, Fargo & Co.'s stage office and chartered two large stages to convey our party to Reno, to start at 7 A.M. the next day. He had suspected these men from the beginning and had played the easy simple-minded trustful man to perfection. He also had the agent call at the hotel and receive all the diamonds and jewels to the value of $40,000 and the watches, money etc. belonging to the company, with orders to forward them to us by their regular express which always was accompanied by an armed guard, for which Mr. B. paid them a heavy insurance.

At 7 o'clock the next morning we started; the ride down was a perilous one. The road cut in the side of the mountain was about ten feet wide, with a broader excavation every mile to serve as a "turn out" for vehicles coming in an opposite direction. Putting a shoe upon one of the wheels and having a strong "break" [sic], the driver started the team of 4 horses upon a full trot which he never abated until we reached the foot of the mountain. The same horses had traveled the road for 3 years, and the driver, trusting to their instinct, did not pretend to guide them but merely held them in check. We arrived at Reno without inter[r]uption. The regular stage, however, was stopped at the foot of the mountain by 4 highwaymen and the passengers robbed. They were the same four men, for while robbing the travelers the fellows frequently uttered the name of "General Tom Thumb" interspersed with oaths against "that mild-mannered easygoing manager."

From Reno we went to Truckee, Dutch Flat, Nevada City, Grass Valley and on to Sacremento [sic] and arrived in San Francisco Aug. 2d. While at Sacremento, Vice-President Colfax, who was on a tour of the state, arrived and received a grand public reception. He sent his card, requesting an interview. We had a pleasant call and enjoyed him very much.

Our reception at St. [sic] Francisco was a perfect ovation. Our entertainments were given at Platt's Hall, capable of holding 2,000 people. Three times a day for a fortnight the hall was filled to repletion. The streets leading from the hotel to the hall were so crowded with ladies and children to see us ride to and fro that they were rendered impassible for vehicles. To quote the expression of an old pioneer, "Them 'ar little folks make more excitement than an airthquake."[36]

We had planned to go through Upper California and Oregon. There was no railway, and if we went by steamer to Portland we should miss many towns between San Francisco and Portland; we determined to make the trip overland. Having obtained two good Concord coaches, ten horses and two expert drivers, we started upon the journey to cross hill, mountain and valley. In going from Suison [*Suisun*] to Silveyville we lost our way. After wandering around for two hours we at length struck the Sacramento River and at half past one we arrived dusty and fatigued. Mr. Bleeker sought the landlady and inquired whether we could have dinner.

"You should have come before," said she sharply. "It was ready at 12 o'clock."

"We lost our road and wandered ten miles out of our course," said Mr. B.

"I can't help that," said she. "Dinner was ready and you'd oughter been here to eat it."

"I regret our delay," said Mr. B., "but *may* we have dinner? We'll take anything."

"'Taint cooked," said she. "What?" inquired Mr. B. "Anything," said she. "*Will* you give us dinner?" said Mr. B. impatiently. "I s'pose so," said she. "Sit down."

Mr. B. called us and we took our seats at the table, which was swarming with flies. After a pause, "Speak up!" exclaimed she. "Don't be afraid; what'll yer take?"

"I'll take that feather duster with which to brush away the flies," said the General, pointing to it.

"No you won't," said she; then addressing a lad, "Bill, brush 'em out." We all felt confused and no one spoke.

"You've got tongues, why don't you use them?" snapped she.

"Give your orders," said Mr. B. to us.

"No orders here!" she exclaimed. "Say what you want: beef or mutton?"

We all expressed our wishes. She disappeared and presently returned, bearing each one's plate which she whirled to them across the table. Mr. B. looked at his dish and remarked, "Madame, I asked

109

you for beef without gravy and you give me mutton swimming in gravy."

"You're awful particular!" said she, snatching the plate. She shortly returned and placed another plate before him with a thump. As she walked away, Mr. B. remarked to me in an undertone, "Is it not a wonder that a person dependent upon the public for support should be so uncivil." She overheard it and, turning sharply, exclaimed, "Eat your dinner now you've got it and let the victuals stop your mouth."

"I don't eat pastry," said the General. "I will take a piece of cheese instead." "Let's see you take it; but you don't take my cheese in this house," replied she with a toss of her head.

We finished our meal in a most unusual silence and demurely retired. We had an excellent supper; but she did everything with a snap. It was amusing to see the male boarders enter the dining room when the bell rang. While she stood bolt upright, her eyes fixed sternly on the door, they entered with bowed heads and glided silently to their seats like so many pupils in a school room. But few words were spoken during the meal, and those only in a whisper. I wondered if in some previous existance [sic] she had been a "school-marm." Rumor had it that her husband slept outside on the balcony and falling off was killed. From our point of view the idea of suicide was tenable.

In going from Marysville to Colusa we had a very narrow escape from a fearful death. Stopping to give the horses water, the gentlemen left the carriage for a stroll and the driver got down to readjust the harness. Just as he detached the two leaders, from some unaccountable fright the two others dashed off with us. Mrs. Bleeker gathered Minnie and myself in her arms and with the calmness of a brave woman awaited death. I could see no hope of escape and so could only follow her example of quiet waiting. Minnie was too young to take in the full horror of the situation and only said to the terrified horses, "I can ride as fast as you can run!" After running nearly a mile, the frightened animals suddenly swerved to the side of the road and, plunging into a fence, destroyed thirty feet of it before one of them fell, thus stopping their onward rush and undoubtedly saving our lives. We all sprang out as the carriage came to a standstill, and then we had time to realize how narrow had been our escape. The experience of that ride will stay in my memory forever.[37]

110

The day following, rain fell continually; and late in the afternoon we reached "Callahan's Ranch," drenched and uncomfortable.[38] We were given tea with gin in it! This antedates the present "afternoon tea" with its soupçon of rum, but it can't have been much worse.

After leaving Red Bluff we came in view of Mount Shasta with its snow-crowned summit. It is over 14,000 feet high. We passed to the westward, a short distance from its base. In going from Trinity Centre to Yreka our course lay over "Scott's Mountain," 9,500 feet high. It was 6 miles to its peak, as the narrow road cut in the side wound around it. To relieve the horses, the men walked beside the coaches. We also, when near the summit, walked a long distance. There was a tollhouse on its peak, as the road had been made by Wells, Fargo & Co. for the purpose of conveying the mail. There was considerable traffic over the road done by 8- and 10-mule teams. While walking, Mrs. Bleeker, Minnie and myself would sometimes leave the road and climb up into the timber where the sides of the mountain were not too precipitatous [sic]. On our reaching the tollhouse, a log cabin, Mr. Bleeker was awaiting us, he having walked ahead alone and had told the tollman who we were. The tollman had a little lunch prepared consisting of tea and nice white bread and fresh butter. He received us very cordially and made an apology for the lunch. "The bread is my own make," said he when we praised it. "You see, I live here all alone, only going down about once a fortnight to get supplies. I can't leave very well in the daytime, and I daren't go out at night on account of the bears and wild animals." "Are there any bears around here?" I inquired. "Lots of 'em," said he, "both grizzlies and cinnamon. The grizzlies has the name, but I think the cinnamon the most ugly customer." I told him that we had climbed into the timber. "Well," said he, "there's not much danger in the daytime, for the noise of the teams keep[s] them away from the road. Sometimes an old she bear when cold and hungry will show herself and frighten horses, which is dangerous business for if they shy they have an ugly tumble, but at night the critters take to the road; it is a good clear run for 'em. I always close my door at nightfall and have those fellows handy in case of need" (pointing to 3 rifles hanging upon a rack). "I have many a night stood in that window when the moon was a shinin' and seen half a dozen of the rascals go down the road. I don't fire at 'em. I'd only wound 'em and that wouldn't do me any good. But as I was goin' to say, it wasn't prudent for you to leave the road." I made up my mind that hereafter I would remain with the coaches. After an hour's rest we descended the mountain on the other side at a more rapid rate, and at 4 P.M. we arrived at "Callahan's Ranch." We remained there overnight, as it rained heavily. The next morning it was clear and cold, and as we looked up at "Scott's" towering form we saw that it was completely covered with snow for some distance below its summit. We continued our journey, stopping every day at some town, large or small, until we reached Portland, Oregon. From there we sailed in the steamship *Oriflamme* for San Francisco. For two days we were amused viewing great numbers of enormous whales, blowing and disporting themselves frequently within a hundred yards of the vessel.

While in Sacremento we had been entertained by Mr. Charles Crocker, the railroad magnate, and on our return to San Francisco we were welcomed and invited to dine by his father, Judge Crocker. We also received and accepted invitations from the Stanifords and were introduced to royal personages from Hawaii, whose pictures with autographs I still have. I little then expected to later welcome their countrymen as citizens of the United States.

The flowers are indescribable, as everybody knows who has been in California, and we were overwhelmed with them till the profusion was bewildering.

We were told that Vice-President Colfax was momentarily expected; and being on the upper veranda and hearing music, Minnie and I ran hastily in the direction of the sound and then scurried back to the centre to see him mount the steps, for we found that instead of passing he was coming to our hotel. I laughingly told Minnie that he was the only man I ever run after. Imagine my consternation when a short time after his card was sent up with a request that we would receive him. He was genial and friendly, and we felt so perfectly at ease with him that I was in constant terror lest Minnie, in a burst of confidence of which she was quite capable, should tell him of our running about the piazza and my remark concerning it. I drew a relieved breath when he bowed himself out of the room without having heard it. Minnie was never a slave to the proprieties and not infrequently took to herself the immunities of the youngest of the party.

112

Chapter 14

DEPARTURE FOR JAPAN. YOKOHAMA. FUJI-YAMA. SAILING
THROUGH THE INLAND SEA. JEDDO. MATSMAI. HAKODADI.
ISLAND OF PAFFENBERG. NAGASAKI.

NOVEMBER 4TH, 1869, we sailed in the Pacific Mail steamship
America, Captain Doane, for Yokohama, Japan. It had been pre-
dicted that an earthquake accompanied by a tidal wave of unusual
severity would be experienced, the effect of which would be felt
many leagues at sea, and ship captains were warned not to leave port.
The morning was very calm, and the state of the atmosphere was
said to be similar to that which preceded the last great earthquake.
However, as announced, the *America* sailed, and the 'quake did not
occur. There were 1,100 Chinamen on board, but such was the
immense capacity of the vessel that few of the cabin passengers were
aware of the fact, as they were all between the two lower decks; a
certain number at a time were allowed on the forecastle to obtain the
fresh air. The vessel carried 12 guns and had a magazine of small
arms and ammunition as a defense against Chinese pirates when we
should reach those waters. Not exactly a pleasant anticipation!

    An incident occurred which gave me a new idea of the Chinese.
Very few had been seen in New England at that time, so finding

myself among so many of them seemed almost as if we had already reached foreign lands. One day there was an outcry "Man overboard." Immediately everybody rushed, and I felt the sickening sense of terror such a cry must always bring. Boats were lowered and the steamer lingered and cruised about till hope was exhausted. Investigation developed the fact that the man was crazed with opium, and when his friends were interrogated they calmly smoked and confessed to seeing him jump to his death; but as "Joss" [39] wanted him, it would have been presumptuous in them to interfere! I mentally determined to take no extra risks when only Chinamen were about, and cherished some doubt as to whether "Joss" really "wanted" the opium-soaked specimen.

The passengers varied, as of course they must, but one to whom I had felt no attraction showed her real kindness of heart when, hearing there was some illness down below among the steerage passengers, [she] said, "Captain, if anything is needed down there, my pocketbook is yours." There was a missionary and his wife, compelled by poverty to go in the steerage. The man had already translated the Bible into the Siamese language, and now after a brief visit home this cultivated, educated man and wife were travelling in the steerage on their way back to carry the gospel to these far-off people. No sooner did this become known than the passengers contributed enough to secure for them a second-class passage, thus giving them the comfort of a private stateroom and greater freedom on deck.

There was also on board an English barmaid who suffered greatly from a peculiar form of toothache. Whenever the surgeon was about, its intensity increased, and in his absence the pain was perceptibly better. Some of the ladies on board were a bit sceptical regarding it, and bets were on between the gentlemen as to whether for the sake of having the surgeon's arm around her she'd go so far as to have a tooth taken out. She did, and the question of whether it was pain or pluck is still open. A sister had married well in Shanghei, and the young woman confidently expected to be similarly successful.

We had little to do besides observe and discuss each other, for in those days fewer steamships or sailing vessels crossed the Pacific, so there was little outside to attract our attention. There was something inexpressibly solemn in sailing day after day over the blue waste, no sign of ship or sail, ourselves but a speck on the waters.

We were twenty-five days in crossing and at one point experienced a terrible cyclone. The storm began near midnight and lasted four hours. Almost everybody gathered in the saloon with the instinct for companionship so common in moments of danger, and when I did not find Mr. or Mrs. Bleeker among [them?] I was filled with apprehension and tried to get to their stateroom; but I didn't have strength to open the door to get out, and everybody was too frightened to assist me. Mr. Bleeker, who had slept through it all, laughed heartily when I told him I had tried to get to them and asked what I supposed I could have done if they had really been in danger. I'm sure I didn't stop to consider that question. I guess I must have felt as the General did when he reached up to shake hands with the boy Prince of Wales, remarking "You have the advantage of me in height, but I feel as big as anybody." [40]

We were quite interested in Brook's Island, because though small and unattractive and uninhabited as well, we were told that the Pacific Mail Steamship Company had deposited a large quantity of coal there for the benefit of any of their steamers which through any unforseen [sic] emergency might get short of fuel. Even in case of a coal strike there's not much danger of its being carried off in baskets.

The Hawaiian flag is a beautiful and showy one, and as we looked at it with admiration we little thought that we should ever see it replaced by the Stars and Stripes, or that the same dear emblem would float over the Phillipines [sic]. Had this been true then, we shouldn't have felt so far from home.

In speaking of the great number of Chinese on board—and it did seem a great number to be going that way, toward China—I have neglected to mention a baby boy that was often allowed to come up on deck. He became a great favorite with my husband, and perhaps because of our size he was less shy of our party than of big people. He played and scampered about with us to the delight of everybody, his father included. This reminds me of one thing in the life of the General which always touched me deeply. He was more fond of children than most and particularly delighted to see them play. "Vinie," he'd say, "I like to watch them play. You know I never had any childhood, any boy-life." And it somehow seemed pathetic to realize its truth. Mr. Barnum took him when only four years old, and from that time he was trained to speak and act like a man. He had, as he said, no childhood, and as he developed into manhood the

115

sense of this loss made him particularly tender of children. Right here it may be said that for some of the bad habits for which General Tom Thumb was blamed, the conditions of his daily life should be counted as extenuation. He was taught to take wine at dinner when only five, to smoke at seven and "chew" at nine. This was a part of the education which supposably fitted him to fill the role he was expected to play. Few would withstand the force of habits so early formed, but I am glad to be able here to say Mr. Stratton had manliness and will power enough to give up these years before he died.[41]

As we approached the shores of Japan our attention was first riveted, as must be that of all comers, on the beautiful mountain Fuji-Yama. A native legend says that one of the early emperors was buried here and that, bursting with its sense of the honor conferred, the mountain immediately sprang into flame and for ages sent forth fire and smoke. If this is true, it was a more dignified form of cremation than that now in vogue in India. One thing is true, I am sure, and that is that the beauty and grandeur of the mountain as it looks today is sufficient excuse for the title "Sacred Mountain." Smooth, symetrical [sic], showing no seams or scars, it towers in calm dignity above all else, visible far out at sea, a landmark for navigators—a shrine for all lovers of the beautiful.

Nearing Yokohama, we were surrounded by sampans— aquatic hacks—and like the hack drivers of those days, they shouted and gesticulated as they surrounded the ship, calling in a high-keyed voice and not hesitating to knock each other overboard in their eagerness to secure passengers. We had no alternative but to submit ourselves to these scantily clothed boat-hack men and be taken ashore in the slim craft they so skillfully managed, for our ship came to anchor three miles from shore and our captain's "gig" had room only for himself and the mails he was bound to deliver. The throng of boatmen chattered and shouted like so many sparrows in a bush.

Stoddard describes some of the drivers he employed as wearing a handkerchief about the loins and a tablecloth on the head. These boatmen lacked the tablecloth, and as we had not yet become accustomed to this form of "undress uniform" which [the] General said was simply uniform undress, our faces betrayed our astonishment and drew peals of laughter from the captain, who shouted as

116

his crew pulled by us, "It's only skinning eels." We did get used to it by and by, but I've always felt great sympathy for the eels. When we were finally bestowed in the hotel, we were told our rooms were "topside," a graphic way of announcing that they were upstairs. As there were no locks or keys, the process of bestowing ourselves therein was accomplished without the conventional bellboy. I roomed with Minnie, as she declared she wouldn't be left alone. Suddenly we saw the door open, and a smiling face appeared to say, "Tea? Likee tea?" Then a second face smiled in: "Blackee boo? Cleanee coat?" Knowing Mr. Stratton's heedlessness in such matters, I hastened to his room just in time to go through his pockets before he yielded his coat to be "cleanee." Our trunks were still on the ship, and it became a problem of some importance when we were to recover coats and boots submitted to these smiling fellows. Again we were importuned to take some tea, and when the boy found himself no longer useful on our floor, he hilariously announce[d] "no topside" and hastened downstairs.

The same evening we gave an entertainment to the Europeans in a new Masonic hall. In all the cities we visited in Japan we had no difficulty in freely going about; although the natives would rush from their shops and follow us sometimes to the number of several hundred, they never annoyed us by crowding upon us. It must be remembered that this was only fifteen years after Commodore Perry's first visit and when an American in the cities of Japan was a rare sight, and a Japanese in America still more rare. They interrogated Mr. Bleeker as to our nationality, pointing and saying "Mellican?" He assenting, they seemed pleased. Our nation seemed the favorite.

The perfect good breeding manifested by these "un-Christianized" Japanese left room for the fear that the efforts of missionaries, however commendable from a religious standpoint, might leave something to be desired in manners if American children were to be taken as an exemplification of Christian etiquette.

While at Yokohama, the U.S. steamer *Oneida* was lying in the harbour, and having made the acquaintance of the officers, we enjoyed much social communion with them. The day of our departure they came on board our vessel to bid us farewell. In parting, many were the wishes exchanged and hopes expressed that we might meet again in our native land, a hope that was soon suddenly destroyed. The *Oneida* was lost in leaving the harbor shortly after, and nearly all of the principal officers perished.

On the afternoon of Dec. 1st, 1869, we embarked on board the steamship *New York*, commanded by that popular officer Captain W. G. Furber, formerly in the service of the Collins line of Liverpool steamers. He was one of the oldest and most experienced captains navigating the Inland Sea, an extremely difficult and dangerous passage requiring great skill and an intimate knowledge of every point, rock and headland. The scenery is beautiful. Jeddo, the capital (now called Tokio) of the empire, is situated on the south of the island of Niphon. A description of one city will answer for all: houses one story in height, streets mostly narrow and tortuous; the greater proportion of houses being used as shops give[s] a busy thriving appearance to every town. Matsmai and Hakodadi on the island of Jesso are exceptions, the streets being wide and regular. At Hioga, containing a population of 25,000, there were at that time but seventy Europeans and only three white females. While in Japan we exhibited before the high officials, the Japanese ladies and the few Europeans to be found in the empire. We were everywhere received with great expressions of kindness and hospitality. When the General's and Commodore's titles were announced by the interpreter, they looked upon them as great personages in our country and extended all the courtesies due "great men." The General always said that, considering their titles, he guessed they were two of the biggest "little" men to be scared up. Whereupon Minnie suggested that if self-approbation was the standard, he was undoubtedly right.

We often saw the Japanese jugglers perform their wonderful tricks, before which Blitz, Herrman and Keller would silently yield the palm. No scenery, no accessories—only squatted on the ground in the open street, silently performing these startling wonders so frequently described by travellers—so utterly unfathomable.[42]

From thence we sailed through the Inland Sea, passing many beautiful islands and approaching Nagasaki through the straits of Corea. Most of these islands are mountainous in the interior, ending in lofty hills as they slope towards the coast, presenting upon the coasts bold cliffs and precipitous headlands. The hills are cultivated to their summits in terraces, while in every little valley between the hills are thriving villages. Near the mouth of the harbor we passed

118

the island of Paffenberg. It is of small dimensions and presents a high precipitous bluff gradually sloping towards the harbor. It is noteworthy as witnessing the destruction of the Jesuit missionaries early in the 16th century. They had introduced Christianity into Japan, but their doctrine was repudiated and the self-sacrificing missionaries cast from the precipices of this island into the sea.

Nagasaki contains a population of 20,000 and is built upon the slopes of hills which encompass a deep commodious bay. The Dutch enjoyed a commerce with this place for over 200 years. But two vessels a year were allowed to enter the harbour and were compelled to land and receive their cargoes at a point two miles from the city. The town covers a very large space; most of the houses except the business portion possess large gardens laid out tastefully with paths, rivulets, bridges, flowers and shrubs. Although many of the streets from the position of the town would be naturally steep, the ascent is modified by flights of stone steps at intervals. The Dutch trading houses contain an extensive variety of the most exquisite china, in the purchase of which I availed myself.

At the hotel we went to inspect Minnie's room.[43] It was well we did, for on the wall we discovered a huge centipede. I say "huge," for that word best describes the impression the creature produced on us. As it was the only specimen I ever saw, I've no means of knowing how it compared with others of its kind. We called a servant to kill it. He came, calmly looked at it and went out, presently returning with a second man. Both inspected it critically but made no move to dispose of it. Our eager demands "Kill it! Kill it!" evoked a surprised stare. Then the two went out, evidently impressed from our manner that something must be done. Returning with two others and a large cloth resembling a sheet, the four of them, holding the sheet by each corner, laid it up against the wall and then, apparently brushing the objectionable insect into it, silently withdrew. Whether regard for our sensibilities came in, or a spirit of cleanliness not observable elsewhere led them to wish to avoid a spot on the partition wall, we were at a loss to conjecture. Certainly they didn't kill it in our presence, but as it was gone we didn't concern ourselves as to its destination. But we were careful to inspect our beds, thinking that if we could stand a smaller insect, we preferred to avoid the larger.

119

Chapter 15

Across the Yellow Sea to China. Shanghae. Appearance in the native Chinese theatres "Kwin-Kwae-Hien," Foe Kein Road, and the "Tong-Kwe-Chin" beside the walls of the old city. Through the China Sea to Hong Kong. Breakfasting with Sir Richard Graves MacDonald, K.C.B. Canton. Macao. Honored by the Portugese [*sic*] Governor-General of Macao. Witnessing a military high mass by invitation of the Governor-General in the Portugese grand cathedral.

Across the "Yellow Sea" to China was our next voyage, and the dirty amber of the water suggested that it was rightly named. The query arose whether the color had washed off the Chinese complexion or into it. At 9 a.m. we entered the mouth of the Yang-tay-Kiang and at 3 p.m. landed at Hong-Que (now known as Hong Kong) opposite Shanghae, with which city it is connected by a strong handsome bridge.

120　　　We were offered the use of a small theatre erected by a club of English merchants for the purpose of amateur theatricals. We had no reason to complain of want of patronage. The excitement amongst the natives, at the sight of the ponies and the carriage as it circulated through the city of Shanghae and such glimpses as they caught of us, daily increased. The patrons of the several Chinese theatres insisted that we should be engaged for their benefit. The first to make application was the manager of the "Kwin-Kwae-Hien," Foe Kein Road, the largest and finest theatre in Shanghae. He was introduced by a European merchant, who assured us that this theatre was the Drury Lane of the city, being under the immediate patronage of the mandarins and other high officials. An arrangement was finally concluded whereby the prices were to be doubled, the manager to furnish an interpreter and to advertise us to his countryman [*sic*] and we to receive seventy percent of the gross receipts. Our ponies and carriage perambulated the streets, followed by quite a procession of Chinamen carrying banners bearing inscriptions in Chinese characters. The banners were of silk and very handsome.

The theatre was located in the heart of the city; the interior was about 80 feet long, 60 feet wide and 40 feet high. A gallery extended all the way around, with the manager's box in the centre facing the stage. The parquet was railed off—about 40 feet square—leaving seats [at] each side, the back ones elevated. Within the railing were a number of tables capable of accommodating four persons, with 4 bamboo chairs to each; the boxes in the gallery contained the same. Upon the tables are placed tea and fruits; and as the ladies indulge in smoking, between the pipe and tea they had something to soothe their minds. These tables are graced by the presence of the small-footed almond-eyed beauties with their attendant *ahmas* or female servants. I observed them exchange courtesies in the following manner. Upon seeing an acquaintance seated at another table, the lady would bow to her, then motion to her *ahmas* who, taking the lady's pipe (a small affair holding about two whiffs of tobacco or a corresponding quantity of opium), would light it, cross to the party indicated [and] place it between the lady's lips. After taking a whiff, the friend bowed an acknowledgement and the attendant would return with the pipe to her mistress. There seemed no hesitation at closing the lips over a pipe that someone else had smoked. Perhaps after accepting tobacco or opium the rest was easy. Almost everyone smoked and there was a great display of pipes; and the air was redolent with the perfume of tea, tobacco, opium, oranges and other fruits.

The stage extended entirely across the building and was devoid

121

little piecee 'oman' good! "

In the evening when we rode to the theatre, within a distance of at least an eighth of a mile of its doors we had to thread our way through lines of sedan chairs and palanquins with their numerous bearers and attendants who having deposited their burdens had retired to give place to others; each attendant being provided with large lighted Chinese lanterns ~~causing such~~ a brilliant illumination *at* the theatre ~~was~~ ~~even more brilliant~~ and during our engagement of several days ~~by~~ *the building* ~~last night but the same~~ was ~~building~~ *lighted* at every entertainment.

The great success attending our appearance excited the other managers and they were all running after Mr Bleeker to make an arrangement but as our time was limited he refused. One manager however was so persistent, his theatre being a rival to the "Kwin-Kwae-Hien," that Mr B. agreed for us to appear at the "Tong-Kwe Chin" theatre for one hour for a stipulated sum, the amount to be paid before 6 PM on the evening of our

appearance. The manager called punctually, bringing with him
several witnesses, and paid the money; but he lingered, apparently in doubt whether, having received the money, we would keep
the appointment. We couldn't but hope that his anxiety was not
founded on any previous experience. At last he said, "Myypayee,
little piecee man no come; Ah!" throwing out his hands indicating ruin. But Mr. Bleeker assured him in "pigeon English,"
that we would be punctual and he left apparently satisfied of
our reliability.

The names they gave us — "little piecee man,
"little piecee 'oman," struck us as very comical though we
could not deny the fitness.

Here we learned that the custom of binding the feet of female children, differed in the different provinces. In the province
where we were it was limited to the oldest daughter in order as it
seemed to insure the having one lady in the family.

A LEAF OF LAVINIA'S AUTOBIOGRAPHY, SHOWING BOTH TYPED AND HAND-
WRITTEN CORRECTIONS AND ADDITIONS MADE DURING HER REVISION. THE
"SHOW-THROUGH" AT THE BOTTOM IS THE ORIGINAL WRITING ON THIS PAGE.

of scenery, but what was lacking in that respect was made up by the most beautiful and elaborate dresses. The number of actors was very great. The manager informed us that he employed 180. [*Here Lavinia indicates a footnote is in order, containing the following information*: Taking into consideration the fact that the performance commences at noon and runs till midnight, and then is continued from day to day for weeks and even months, it is evident that a less number might become wearied if the audience didn't. And then if, in their peculiar national methods, it became necessary to decapitate a few, there would be plenty of understudys.] Their plays consist of a history of some celebrated emperor or other great personage from birth to death: his public acts, wars, love passages all are represented. It is like a book that cannot be read in a day—so many chapters are represented today, so many tomorrow until finished—a single play sometimes occupying several weeks. The stage is a public instructor in national history. [*Another note*: From one point of view this is an agreeable method of learning history, but considering the time occupied there'd be opportunity for a pupil to die of old age before his historical education was completed. This discounts the modern "continuous performance."[44]] At the entrance and exit of every character their inharmonious instruments squeaked doleful approbation. As in the days when Shakespeare wrote, the Chinese allow no women on the stage (bald-headed men are not plentiful in China).[45] Female parts are taken by men, and so dramatically skilful are they that every motion of their hands, every movement of their bodies, is like a woman['s].

Our performance evidently gave great satisfaction. My songs particularly called forth great applause; the audience at their conclusion chatted, laughed, nodded and expressed extreme delight. Commodore's dancing, drumming and comicalities excited their risibilities; and the General in his character sketches was received in open-mouthed wonder. We also performed a pantomime which had been arranged for us, at which they laughed heartily. Mr. B. took a dozen little Chinese children upon the stage to compare their size with Minnie['s]—the great difference excited their wonder—after which he passed them off the stage, retaining a little boy five years old who towered above Minnie. He was elegantly dressed in silk with the most elaborate embroidery in gold; he had a pigtail that almost touched the floor. Mr. B. placed Minnie's hand in the little

123

fellow's hand and whispered to her to walk 2 or 3 times across the stage with him. The boy strutted about with her to the immense delight of the audience, and when Mr. B. handed him down the child was seized, caressed and passed from one to another as one who had been highly honored.

At the conclusion of the performance there was a general rush to the stage by the audience, but they were soon brought under control and the ladies were granted the first privilege. They patted our hands and our feet, chattering and exclaiming "Ah! good! little piecee 'oman! good!"

In the evening when we rode to the theatre, within a distance of at least an eighth of a mile of its doors we had to thread our way through lines of sedan chairs and palanquins with their numerous bearers and attendants, who having deposited their burdens had retired to give place to others, each attendant being provided with large lighted Chinese lanterns, causing a brilliant illumination. At the theatre the scene was even more brilliant, and during our engagement of several days the building was filled at every entertainment.

The great success attending our appearance excited the other managers, and they were all running after Mr. Bleeker to make an arrangement; but as our time was limited, he refused. One manager, however, was so persistent, his theatre being a rival to the "Kwin-Kwae-Hien," that Mr. B. agreed for us to appear at the "Tong-Kwe-Chin" theatre for one hour for a stipulated sum, the amount to be paid before 6 P.M. on the evening of our appearance. The manager called punctually, bringing with him several witnesses, and paid the money; but he lingered, apparently in doubt whether, having received the money, we would keep the appointment. We couldn't but hope that his anxiety was not founded on any previous experience. At last he said, "My payee, little piecee man no come—Ah!" throwing out his hands indicating ruin. But Mr. Bleeker assured him in "pigeon [sic] English" that we would be punctual, and he left apparently satisfied of our reliability. The names they gave us— "little piecee man," "little piecee 'oman"—struck us as very comical, though we could not deny the fitness.

124

Here we learned that the custom of binding the feet of female children differed in the different provinces. In the province where we were it was limited to the oldest daughter in order, as it seemed, to insure the having one lady in the family.

We arrived at the theatre, located in the French concession, at 8 o'clock, and forcing our way through the crowd reached the door of entrance. We went to a room at the rear of the stage and found about fifty persons, some dressing for the stage, others taking refreshments, having fulfilled their share of the performance. A curtain was hung in one corner of the room for our accommodation. Nine o'clock came, the hour appointed for our appearance. The play was in progress. Mr. B. saw the manager and told him it was time and we were ready. He only grinned, nodded and disappeared; he evidently wanted to delay for some reason. Half past nine [and] still the play went on. Mr. B. endeavoured to explain to the actors that they must resign the stage to us, but they pretended not to understand and only nodded and grinned. At length 10 o'clock came and yet they made their entrances and exits. We all became out of patience. "When *are* we going to appear?" inquired the General.

"In a moment," exclaimed Mr. Bleeker.

There was a grand scene in progress; about 30 actors were upon the stage. The Emperor and court were in grand council; there appeared to be some important matter brought before the Emperor for his decision. His magnificent highness was apparently uttering a withering rebuke to one portion of the council when Mr. Bleeker rushed upon the stage; the actors stared in an amazement, shared by the audience. Mr. B. shouted, "Little piecee man, little piecee 'oman! makee show all samee like dis. Savee?" Still the actors stared but did not stir. "Get out!" Mr. Bleeker again shouted, and seizing the play-Emperor pulled him from his throne, pushed him to the door and shoved him through the opening, then hustled the whole crowd after him. Evidently such vigorous English as this was easily comprehended, and the later ones stood not upon the order of their going but went at once in evident fear lest the "Mellican man" should address himself to them. I stood in fear and trembling.

It was a wonder they did not take summary vengeance upon Mr. B. By pretending not to understand him at first, they thought to delay our appearance, and thus they would get through their work a little earlier. We returned to Hong-Que at midnight. It was an eerie hour and a quaint, uncanny sort of ride, feeling ourselves at the mercy of these narrow-eyed natives. A strange country, stranger people and the thought of our recent rather high-handed experience in the theatre all combined to give that midnight ride a prominence in our memories which time cannot efface.

While in China we visited several of the mandarins' residences by invitation, and I now have an elegant set of elaborately carved chessmen, fans, paper knives, sandalwood boxes, fans and other articles too numerous to mention given to my husband, my sister or myself. It is said that the Hoang Ho River (Yellow River) is depositing yellow clay so rapidly that it is thought it will unite China and Japan in three hundred centuries. We thought we wouldn't wait, so we sailed from Shanghae Dec. 17th, 1869, in the steamship *Venus*, Captain Crowell. The following places were in the route: Ningpo, Foochoo, Amoy and Swatow. They contained but few Europeans. In these places the startled natives couldn't understand the phenomena we presented and imagined we were to bring them bad luck in some way. They chattered and gesticulated, and their looks became alarming. Some who had mastered some English exclaimed, "Why come? No good! Bring evil!" Our guide harangued them, assuring them that God had sent us as good omens, and then he waved his hands and "shooed" them off, precisely, as Minnie said, like a "woman shooing chickens." "Only," added the Commodore, "he hasn't an apron to shake at them." A terrible high sea and a ship that rolled fearfully did not detract from the pleasure of the voyage while in the company of such an agreeable captain; we were the only passengers.

The day after our arrival at Hong Kong we received an invitation by letter, delivered to us by the American consul Colonel Goulding, from Sir Richard Graves McDonald, K.C.B., to breakfast with him the next day at 12 o'clock M. We accepted and were most agreeably entertained at the Government House. The following appeared in the *China Mail* of December 22d:

> His Excellency Sir Richard Graves MacDonald, K.C.B., Governor-General of Hong Kong, Vice-Admiral etc. this morning did himself the honor of entertaining at breakfast General Thomas Thumb and suite. The entertainment was given at Government House and the American consul was present. In the absence of any journal devoted to fashionable

intelligence we venture to record this fact, and we do so purely in the interests of fashionable society. We are not aware that there is anything in the world of Hong Kong that is at present more deserving of notice. It is the most remarkable event since the Prince has departed.

We gave our performances in the town hall to large and fashionable audiences.

We next proceeded to Macao in an American-built steamer. As we approached the city we threaded our way through hundreds of junks, many of them war vessels. The island was given to the Portugese by the Chinese government for the assistance it had received from them in clearing the neighbouring coasts from Chinese pirates in 1536. The whole circuit of the settlement is about 8 miles, with a population of 33,000 Chinese. Think of that, ye New England farmers!

While at Macao we had a call from Captain Constanius, the wonderfully tattooed man. He was, I think, a Greek, who had been tattooed in captivity and, having escaped, proposed to make his misfortune serve toward his support.[46] He was anxious to visit America and called on us in the hope that we could graft him on to our party and thus he could get to America, and his grief was voluable [sic] when he found that could not be done. How he managed it we never knew, but he reached this country, as the public will remember; and when on our return we went to Barnum's Museum, he, the tattooed man, recognizing us, burst into almost tearful welcome, reaching out both hands to us and crying "Maceo, Maceo!" We reminded him of his far-off home, and his emotion was really touching.

We exhibited in the Teatro Don Pedro d. V. His Excellency the Governor-General honored us with an invitation to accept his hospitality at the Government House. He also came in state to our entertainment. At its conclusion he arose and publicly thanked us for the pleasure he had received, his son interpreting his words.

The next day being Sunday, a military high mass was to be celebrated, and the Governor invited us to be present. At 10 o'clock the next morning we went to the cathedral, a massive building containing some fine old paintings. The high altar glittered with silver and gold. We were assigned seats which had been prepared for us near the altar and close beside the raised platform of His Excellency. Presently the music of the band announced the approach of the military. His Excellency entered followed by his suite and, bowing low to us, took his seat upon the chair emblazoned with the Royal Arms. The band marched into the gallery opposite the altar, and the regiment of soldiers entered at the main doors, formed company front at the entrance and advanced in that form, filling the immense nave, the butts of their muskets ringing upon the stone floor as they came to a halt. Twelve of them, with fixed bayonets, advanced within the railing and formed six each side of the altar. During the service the music of the band was substituted for that of the organ, while at intervals the clear notes of the bugle echoed through the building as signals to the soldiers to kneel and rise according to the requirements of the service. Those who have witnessed a similar service at St. Peter's, Rome, or in any of the cathedrals upon the Continent can fully appreciate the feeling it inspires.

Returning to Hong Kong, we gave an entertainment in the Portuguese theatre and were afterward entertained by the National Club in their magnificent ballroom.

Almost every fruit known in Europe may be found in China. Some, from lack of proper cultivation, are inferior. One which to me was peculiar, called "letchee," [is] about as large as a walnut with a rich brown husk. The natives take it with their tea in preference to sugar; it has a pleasant acid taste. It is sometimes exported in a dried state, wrinkled like a prune. I have since seen it several times in New York. Another fruit is the "petchee." It is like a water lily, to the root of which is attached a white substance enveloped in a red skin; this white substance is edible and is said to possess the strange property of rendering copper very brittle. In view of the recent discovery that an acid (tauric) made from tauric moss will make the finer metals "pliable as putty," this claim may not be improbable but only add to the evidence that China was a leader in many arts even before the Christian Era.

A portly Tom Thumb and Lavinia pose on a theatrical balcony.

Tom Thumb in his Knights Templar uniform

A PENSIVE LAVINIA POSES IN HER WIDOW'S WEEDS SHORTLY AFTER THE
DEATH OF TOM THUMB.

Baron Ernesto Magri, Lavinia, and her second husband Count Primo Magri

Lavinia in white

Count Primo and Baron Ernesto Magri in one of their burlesque skits

DETAIL OF A PHOTOGRAPH OF LAVINIA AND COUNT MAGRI TAKEN AT THE
SOUTHERN NEW ENGLAND COUNTRY FAIR ON 15 SEPTEMBER 1914

THE COUNTESS M. LAVINIA
MAGRI, FORMERLY MRS. GEN-
ERAL TOM THUMB.

THE GRAVES OF TOM THUMB AND LAVINIA AND THE STRATTON FAMILY
MONUMENT, CROWNED BY A STATUE OF TOM THUMB, IN BRIDGEPORT'S
MOUNTAIN GROVE CEMETERY

Chapter 16

SINGAPORE. ENTERTAINED BY THE MAHARAJAH OF JOHORE.
ISLAND OF PENANG IN STRAITS OF MALACCA. ACROSS
THE INDIAN OCEAN. CEYLON. POINT DU GALLE. COLOMBO.
KANDY. A VISIT TO THE "TEMPLE OF THE SACRED TOOTH."
THE "GOD BUDDAH [sic]."

ON TUESDAY, DECEMBER 28TH, we sailed in the Peninsular and
Oriental Steamship Company's steamer *Emu*, Captain Babot, for
Singapore, Penang and Point du Galle. Our voyage down the China
Sea was pleasant and we landed at Singapore the following Sunday.
Singapore formerly belonged to the Kingdom of Johore in Malacca,
but in 1824 the English purchased it for 60,000 Spanish dollars and a
life annuity of $24,000, securing not only the sovereignty of the
island but also the sea, straits and islands within an area of ten
geographical miles. They established the provincial government at
Penang, where the governor now resides. The maharajah lives in
Singapore, he preferring that city, and has a handsome palace there.
Shortly after our arrival His Highness came on board with the
commodore of the station and was introduced to us. At 8 o'clock in
the evening, having accepted his invitation, we visited his palace and
were courteously received. His costume was an admixture of native

129

and European; he spoke English fluently. He had visited England and had been the guest of the Royal Family. His palace was furnished in Oriental style intermixed with much that was European. After being introduced to his household, excepting his wife and daughter, we were given refreshments. He then ordered an attendant to conduct the ladies to his wife and the princess, and turning to the General said, "I regret that our custom debars me the pleasure of introducing yourself, Commodore and Mr. Bleeker, but I hope education will in time make a change in that custom."

A few minutes after, the attendant returned and spoke to him in his native tongue. He again said, "My wife's curiosity breaks down the barrier; she wishes to see the General and Commodore." They were therefore conducted into her presence. The gentlemen always boasted that they had been admitted to the private apartments of "Mrs. Rajah," and if Minnie and I had not been present to know the facts there's no guessing the limit of their vain boasting. We were much pleased with the "Ranee" and her daughter. The little princess was 14 and had 14 attendants, one for each year of her existence, the eldest of her own age, the youngest 18 months and just able to toddle around, looking more as if the child should have an attendant. If that sort of thing was to continue, the retinue consequent on a long life might become embarrassing. Upon our return to the ship, Minnie remarked, "I have often heard the expression 'dressed to death and barefooted.' I think it will apply to the Rajah's wife and daughter." They were splendidly dressed—their ears, nose[s], fingers, arms and ankles blazing with diamonds and other jewels, and not the sign of a shoe or stocking. But then, if they had worn shoes there would have been no place to display the toe-rings etc. which adorned their feet.

Singapore being within a few miles of the equator, the inhabitants are not addicted to wearing furs, and it has been said that this city is the hottest on earth. I feel no disposition to dispute the statement. Owing to its climate, vegetation is luxurious and fruit superabundant. When one can buy a pineapple ripened on its own stalk for a cent, or a dozen oranges or bananas, two cocoanuts, etc. etc., one needs no doctor to advise of their hygienic value.

In approaching the harbor, the water swarmed with canoes from which the occupants would dive for pennies tossed in by the passengers, till the surface of the water seemed only a mass of rapidly disappearing tawny legs and feet, transformed below and reappearing as grinning heads with the money firmly gripped in the teeth. The style of clothing worn hardly admits of pockets. You've heard the story of the Irishman who was interrogated, "Pat, why don't you buy a trunk?" "What for?" was the reply. "To put your clothes in." "And go naked!" These fellows probably owned a trunk.

We exhibited in the European portion of the city. On Tuesday, after taking "tiffin" [*lunch*] with His Highness and making a farewell call upon his wife, she presenting each of us with a handsome present as a memento, we left Singapore and proceeded to Penang in the Straits of Malacca. Georgetown, the capital, is quite a large town, having a population of 50,000. Penang is sometimes called "Prince of Wales Island," and by the natives "Pulo Penang" or "Betel Nut Island." It is only sixteen miles long and half as wide. We visited a famous waterfall which came tumbling down the rocks several hundred feet. Ferns grow there to an enormous size, and we could scarce walk a dozen steps without treading upon the "sensitive plant." It gave me a sort of heartache to see the shy leaves fold themselves together, as if our careless feet had hurt them and they had no voice to cry out their pain or warn us against trespass. After picking from the tree betel nuts, nutmegs, mangosteens and many other fruits new to us, and having received a call from the Governor, we were ready to depart for Ceylon.

We arrived at Point du Galle January 11th, 1870. Point du Galle was then used as the calling station for steamers between Suez, India, China and Australia. We gave three entertainments in the military barracks.

[*The following paragraph, an addition made by Lavinia while revising her narrative, occurs on a later leaf of the manuscript, where it is evidently out of place. In fact, as a reading of Bleeker's work reveals, it is meant to apply to the party's experiences at Point du Galle and not, as Lavinia writes, to their later accommodations at Colombo.*]

At Colombo [*Point du Galle*] we found a fine hotel kept by an Englishman. The rooms were all that could be desired in appointments. Our surprise at finding a sheet spread on the dining table was only equalled when we found the tablecloth doing duty as a sheet on our bed. Things seemed to have evened up. When we interviewed the landlady in relation to exchanging the pillowcase we found beside our washbowl for a towel, she loudly bewailed her inability to make "these people" have any idea of the proper use of things. One of them having spilled gravy on the floor and being bidden to wipe it up, she said she found him calmly wiping it up with a table napkin, which he then wrung into the teapot. We examined our plates with some care before eating. They were the hollow "hot-water plates" with a cork, much in use in those days, and our discoveries led us to comprehend the old adage "Ignorance is bliss."

On the 17th we left "Galle" for Colombo, the capital of Ceylon, 72 miles distant, having chartered two mail coaches for the purpose. There were relays of horses every six miles, as they were driven at a full run between stations. Our coach was driven by a native accompanied by a single guard with a brass horn. It was the guard's duty to clear the road of native bullock and buffalo teams so as to afford an uninterrupted way. Most of the natives who were clothed at all were in white. The others were of necessity in perpetual black. It was what the present-day advertisers might call "fast black," but evidently most of them felt some hesitancy at subjecting it to the vicissitudes of washing. Our guard wore the conventional black, and as he was unimpeded by clothing he trotted or ran ahead of our coach all the long way, apparently suffering nothing from fatigue and evidincing [sic] no especial exertion. It struck me as a point made for vegetarians, for we well knew these people ate no meat. The road was hard and level as a floor and runs the entire distance within an eighth or quarter of a mile of the sea.

This drive, where the blue sky overhead seemed akin to the blue of the sea on the one hand, and where on the other side were groves of cocoanuts, palms and plantains, giving through them glimpses of villages and homes with the whole air of foreign and tropical unusualness, is one of the most beautiful pictures in my memory. Whenever the coach stopped, as it frequently did, even our driver held spellbound by the beauty of the scene, the natives brought cocoanut milk for us to drink, and we found it very different from the insipid stuff we used to drain from the cocoanuts our mother bought at home and which we vainly tried to think was good

132

as we sipped it from a china cup. "Circumstances alters [*sic*] cases," quoted Minnie as she relinquished the fragrant cup of ivory-lined cocoanut shell just broken open for her benefit. The beggars were oppressive. Halt, lame and blind, as well as many less apparently distressed, haunted us like ghosts and made shadows on the otherwise perfect picture of paradise. When the General suggested that these beggars had adopted the style of clothing said to have been in vogue in the Garden of Eden, no one dissented, but one voice suggested that probably fig leaves were less plenty [*sic*] in Ceylon.

It may be explained here that "athletics" had not then become fashionable in America, and serving afternoon tea to bare-legged gentlemen in undervests and abbreviated drawers after a "varsity race" was a branch of our education which had been neglected. Hence our first acquaintance with these scantily clad natives had a spice of the unusual. The males allow their hair to grow long and hang down their backs, sometimes twisting it up like a woman and securing it with a tortoise-shell comb. This, together with their peculiar dress, gives them an oddly feminine look, and the gentlemen of the party professed to a shyness which seriously interrupted the duties of their valets. Male and female, old and young, chew the betel nut, which dyes their mouth[s] almost blood-red. Soon as we had changed horses and dashed off, the lame and halt, blind and dumb recovered their faculties, after having begged piteously to us for money, and pursued us for some distance beyond the village; their long hair streaming and their mouths wide open, revealing the red interiors, conveyed to us the impression of fiendish cannibals drunk with human blood, pursuing fresh victims. At noon we stopped one hour for dinner at a bungalow. We saw a number of large serpents stretched upon the trunks of fallen trees, sunning themselves or wriggling away as we approached. It is said one can get used to anything, and we were in a fair way to get used to snakes; but when a very large python crossed the road directly in front of the horses—so near that we all uttered involuntary exclamations of alarm—we were willing to forego the necessary experience.

At half past 4 P.M. we reached the city gate. The city is well fortified, being surrounded by a high wall and deep ditch built by the Dutch. In 1505 the Portuguese fleet entered at this place and the people were favorably received by the natives; but becoming avaricious in their commercial relations and endeavouring to suppress the native religion, Buddhism, the people became aroused and, receiving assistance from the Dutch who had opened a trade with them, drove the Portugese out of the island in 1603. The Portugese, however, retained a hold in Colombo. This the Dutch captured in 1656. The natives, in return for their assistance, ceded the most valueable [sic] districts to the Dutch; this they afterwards regretted, and in their efforts to recover them a war broke out and the natives were driven to the interior. Finally, by treaty the English took possession and in 1815 subjugated the whole of the island by the capture of the Cingalese King of Kandy. When in Kandy, we visited this king's former palace and saw his grandson, the last survivor of the family. There is still in the interior a semi-barbarous race numbering about 12,000 called "Weddas." They depend upon the chase for a living. There were at that time on the island only 7,000 whites and a million and a half of natives. The thick forests are seldom visited; they swarm with wild beasts, elephants, boars, leopards, monkeys, alligators, serpents and reptiles of all kinds.

We performed in the barracks to an admixture of Europeans, Mahommedans, Moors, Dutch, Portuguese, Parsees and Cingalese. The varieties of color in their different costumes, to say nothing of complexions, presented quite a picturesque appearance. Our quarters were at the Royal Hotel, a Chinaman the manager, the servants Cingalese. The merit next to godliness was unknown to them.

On the 17th we went to Kandy. One of the few railroads we encountered was here from Colombo to Kandy built by the English government at a cost of £150,000. The city being in the mountains, there are many steep grades to ascend. Native labor was used in the construction of this railway, and it is said it cost one life for every sleeper laid. The engineers and contractors, finding the process of filling in and grading very slow when all the earth was conveyed from point to point in baskets carried upon the head, imported a shipload of wheelbarrows. The natives took them because directed so to do, but it is left to the imagination to picture the disgusted astonishment of the contractors when it was found that, laying aside the baskets, the laborers after filling the barrows had mounted the unwieldy things on their heads and trudged calmly off to empty them as they had previously emptied the baskets.

134

The scenery is very picturesque. The lowlands are covered with rice fields; and plantains, palms and cinnamon trees are plenty.

In the north palms abound, while in the south it is said there are twenty million cocoanut trees and coffee everywhere.

Apparently in close proximity to Kandy, a valley however of several thousand feet lying between, is "Bible Mount," resembling in appearance an open Bible upon a pulpit. Adam's Peak, which is about 7,500 feet high, terminates in a striking-looking rock; and to this rock pilgrims journey to worship a colossal footprint said to be that of "Amam," who according to their belief was created there. There is a variety of opinion, however, concerning it. The Buddhists call it the footstep of Buddah, the Brahmanist says of Brahma or Siva, the Mahommedans of Adam, the Chinese of Fo, while the Portugese call it the footprint of Saint Thomas. "You takes your choice," says Minnie, and the Commodore stoutly affirmed it must be that of Gen. Washington. At any rate, pilgrimages are made to it, and the betel leaf is exchanged as a sign of peace.

Kandy is a miserable town surrounded by a mud wall. Its location, however, is pleasant and healthy; and doubtless that explains the fact that during the hot weather the Governor and [his] suite leave Colombo and come here, thus giving it the distinction of being practically the capital part of the year. It has been much improved since the railway was constructed. We were invited to a "kenip" and accepted, to find it was what at home is called a raffle. The object raffled, or should I say "kenipped," was a watch, which Minnie won.

One of the richest Buddhist temples in Ceylon is located here. It is called Dalada Malagana [*Maligawa*] or "Temple of the Sacred Tooth." With a judicious distribution of "bucksheesh," a native was persuaded to conduct us thither. Entering through a narrow gateway in a solid stone wall, we stood in a large square court, in the centre of which was the temple. Upon the wall were two men in dark brown gowns blowing blasts upon conch shells as a notification that Buddaha [*sic*] was being fed. The sacred portion of the temple stands upon an oblong platform of stone five feet above the level of the court. Ascending some steps upon the outside of the building, we entered a door leading into a large square room. By this time quite a number of worshippers had gathered around us. Amongst them was a Musselman [*sic*] who had followed us through the gate; he could speak broken English and we did not repulse him, thinking he might be useful perhaps as an interpreter. Passing through a deep arch at

135

the further end of the room, we emerged into a narrow apartment at the end of which was a large opening or doorway. Before this doorway hung white silk curtains with festoons of yellow flowers at the top; these curtains concealed the entrance to the sacred apartment containing Buddaha. Our native conductor had left us [as] soon as we had entered the first apartment, and the crowd held themselves aloof, not venturing within the sacred precinct. We consulted together a moment whether it would be prudent to attempt an entrance into the sacred presence of the great god, observing the great reverence and fear expressed in their actions by the natives who halted before following so far. We inquired of the Mussulman if we might venture. He evidently was anxious to get a sight himself. "Me tink all right," replied the Mussulman. "Well, here goes," said Mr. Bleeker. "If we get into trouble I'll trust to my wits to get us out of it." So he advanced, seized the curtains, drew them aside and was confronted by two priests dressed in long yellow silk gowns and having narrow yellow bands around their foreheads; behind them hung heavy rich yellow silk curtains. They looked at Mr. B. in amazement and anger and raised their hands, whether in holy horror or to strike him we could not tell, but he stood firmly confronting them. For a moment it formed quite a dramatic picture. Then Mr. B. slowly stepped aside and with a gesture drew their attention towards us. Their eyes followed his motion and then fixed upon us in wonderment. One of them disappeared and returned with two more priests. The Mussulman now became useful. "Tell them," said Mr. B. to him, "that we came from a far-off country and we wish to look upon and bow before the great god Buddah." "We'll do all but the bowing," said Minnie, in whom the blood of our Pilgrim ancestors was always rampant.

The Mussleman [*sic*] explained our wishes and received a reply which he interpreted to us as "God eat, no see," which we learned meant that Buddha was feasting and desired no witnesses. Here was an evidence of good breeding hardly to be expected, but recognizing the reasonableness of the exclusion we waited nearly fifteen minutes, being constantly subjected to the scrutiny of several priests who peered at us from behind the curtain. "If I were Buddha," said Minnie, "I would discharge every one of you for neglect of duty at mealtime. Go and wait upon him properly and ask him to postpone the dessert, for we are in a hurry."

136

The priest hearing her voice smiled and nodded as if he understood, and almost at the same moment an aged priest drew aside the outer curtain and motioned for us to enter. There was a massive door which stood open immediately behind the outer curtains; the inner curtains were suspended at a sufficient distance to allow the door to open and shut. This door was sheathed completely in silver, with beautifully embossed figures of birds, beasts and flowers, and had heavy silver hinges. Entering through the inner curtains, we stood in the great "presence." The apartment was about 20 feet long and 15 feet wide. Across the room was a strong iron cage, the floor of which was 3 feet high. Within this cage sat the god. The bars of the cage were three quarters of an inch in diameter. A door upon one side of the cage was secured with a strong bolt and padlock. In front of the cage was a solid silver table covered with large white and yellow flowers which emitted a delicious perfume. The remains of the feast, which consisted apparently of rice, were strewn around. I imagine it was the priests who in the matter of eating were proxies for the god. A number of silver vessels containing cocoanut oil were suspended from the ceiling, and several candles in silver candlesticks were burning upon the table.

We modestly stopped in the middle of the room, but the old priest motioned us to approach nearer. We perceived that the god's shyness did not extend to receiving strangers. Upon that invitation we walked directly to the bars. The god was of solid gold, about three feet high in a sitting posture, and was rather hideous in appearance. It was covered with jewels and gold chains and other ornaments. A cluster of immense diamonds, sapphires, rubies and emeralds displayed in the form of a bird six inches long was upon its breast. Upon every available space similar jewels, interspersed with pearls, amethysts and topaz, added their beauties. The jewels alone are estimated to be worth £3,000,000 sterling ($15,000,000); the heavy bars are a precaution not so much to prevent the god getting out, as it might seem, but to prevent thieves from getting in. We expressed our admiration to each other. The old priest was so pleased at the admiration we evinced that, thrusting his arm through the bars, he held one of the lighted candles close beside the figure to afford us a better view. We took a long survey. As we were about to depart, two priests advanced and hung long wreaths of yellow flowers around our necks. Mr. Bleeker gave the old priest a handful

137

of "bucksheesh." As we walked away, the Mussulman pulled Mr. B.'s arm and said, "Dey tink God dat shape," pointing to the image and laughing derisively. "Dam fool! Dey tink dat ting eat—dam fool, ha! ha! ha! God see dat ting, he laugh too, ha! ha! ha! dam fool." Then making a grimace at the figure, "You not God—you dam fool! dam fool!" Fearing he might do something to excite the priests, Mr. B. seized and pushed him from the room. Upon each side of the outer room was a large box about four feet square with an opening like a money box in the top. The Mussulman volunteered the information that upon certain festive days "dey bring gold, silver—fill dem box two, tree times a day—tousand pounds—dam fool!" Evidently his English had not been acquired at the missionary Sunday school.

We received an invitation to visit the palace of the last King of Kandy (sometimes called "Kandi") situated 5 miles from the city. We were welcomed by his grandson. He had sent to the forest 20 miles distant and ordered a dozen elephants to be brought in for our amusement. He possessed a large herd and employed them in rolling and carrying timber. Shortly after our arrival we heard the tinkling of their bells as they descended the road, and soon they drew up in line before us and saluted by kneeling and raising their trunks in the air. After going through a most wonderful performance under the direction of their "mahouts" or drivers, far surpassing anything I had ever seen in a circus in this country, they again saluted and returned to the forest. Cocoanuts were plucked, the milk poured into bowls and offered us to drink. We found it very refreshing. Bidding farewell to our host, we returned to the city and gave our entertainments in the English Library building. From thence we returned to Colombo, where we took our coaches for Point du Galle.

His Excellency Sir Hercules Robinson had left the day previous for Galle. The road along the route was decorated with festoons of flowers, beautiful arches and various devices. All of which, done for his benefit, administered no less to our pleasure. "Honors are easy!" exclaimed the Commodore, and we rode along the flower-bestrewn way in most jolly appreciation. But we sang a different tune when, after passing His Excellency, who travelled slowly as became his state, we reached the bungalow and were informed that all available food had been placed on His Excellency's table and we could dine on "biscuit" and water or go hungry. It is due to Sir

Hercules to add that when he found that our party was there he sent his card with a cordial invitation to dine with him; but as the formalities to be observed would occupy more time than we could spare from our journey, we were compelled to decline, though, as the General said, "our hearts accepted." "Stomachs rather," said Minnie. When the landlord presented his bill, on which we were charged for full "dinner," our treasurer energetically quoted the language of our Mahommedan friend at Buddah's temple and settled the account by his own standard of the prices of crackers and cold water.

Chapter 17

VOYAGE TO AUSTRALIA. A TOUR OF THE COLINIES [*sic*], COM-
PRISING A LAND TRAVEL OF 5,300 MILES. CROSSING A PORTION
OF THE GREAT DESERT. NARROW ESCAPE FROM DROWNING
WHILE CROSSING A DEEP AND RAPID RIVER. VISIT TO VAN
DIEMAN'S [*sic*] LAND. PERILOUS VOYAGE. OVERLAND TO
SYDNEY. HIS ROYAL HIGHNESS THE DUKE OF EDINBURGH
OUR GUEST.

JANUARY 28TH, 1870, we sailed from Point du Galle for Australia in
[the] P. & O. steamship *Malta*, Captain Skottowe. After a pleasant
voyage, on the morning of February 16th the *Malta* entered the
narrow passage one and a half miles across called "The Heads" and
steamed across Port Phillip Bay, a splendid landlocked sheet of water
30 miles either way, and cast anchor in Hobson's Bay, the harbor of
Melbourne.

Melbourne might be called the Chicago of the Orient. Founded
in 1837, in 17 years its population was 100,000. When we were there
it had reached 170,000, including its suburbs Collingwood, Richmond, Kew etc.

We opened at Polytechnic Hall on the 21st to a full house, and
for a month the hall was packed day and evening with enthusiastic

audiences. It was a repetition of our San Francisco experience. The streets were thronged daily to see us ride to and from the hall.[47] The Polytechnic was a very fine and convenient hall, and its proprietor, Hon. Dr. L. L. Smith, M.P., was a most courteous, genial companion and warm-hearted friend. His excellent lady deserved the highest encomiums. When leaving the Colonies, there were no persons from whom we parted with greater regret than Dr. Smith and wife. He possessed an excellent racing stable and had been successful upon the turf. Having on the place at that time two fine colts, he named them respectiv[e]ly "Lavinia" and "Minnie"; they both won afterwards several important races. Dr. Smith becoming a happy father shortly after our arrival, the new baby was named Minnie Lavinia and I stood godmother at its christening.

A complimentary benefit having been tendered by the leading citizens of Melbourne to Prof. Robert Heller, the celebrated prestid[i]gitateur, to take place at the Theatre Royal, the largest theatre in Australia (since destroyed by fire), he applied to us, as old friends, to appear on the occasion.[48] The performance was to consist of prestidigitation by Mr. Heller; operatic selections, vocal and instrumental, by popular artists; [and] to conclude with the drawing-room entertainment by Gen. Tom Thumb and party. One hour before the commencement the theatre was filled, and there was a mass of people upon the street unable to gain admittance. The same scene was enacted at the Polytechnic, where we were to give our performance at the hall the first part of the evening—the overflow from both places filling all the other places of amusement. When we appeared, such a shout of welcome we had seldom received; gentlemen cheered and the ladies waved their handkerchiefs. There were over three thousand five hundred persons within the walls. They filled the orchestra, they sat upon the stage, they hung upon the proscenium columns, they climbed from the galleries and sat upon the figures supporting the front of the private boxes. It was indeed a most flattering reception.[49]

There being at that time but a very few railways in Australia, and they running but a short distance from Melbourne, Mr. Bleeker engaged two coaches from Cobb & Co. (the pioneer stage co. proprietors) and eight horses with which to traverse the country. We visited over twenty towns before reaching Ballerat [*Ballarat*], where we proposed to stop. Ballerat is the town first noted in the gold

141

digger's world. Gold has been found in lesser quantities in other parts of Australia, but at Ballerat the "find" was so wonderful that the news spread all over the world and brought hither a population of gold seekers and their accompanying traders etc. which eclipsed even our "forty-niners" in California. To commemorate our visit to Ballerat, my husband had a bracelet made of native gold and suitably inscribed as a present to Minnie from him and myself. It is marked June 2d, 1870. The color is a trifle paler than the California ore. It brings her and those happy days so forcibly to my mind that I am seldom without it.

We remained here three weeks, visiting by invitation the various charitable institutions. In fact, throughout the Colonies there is scarce a town but supports a local charity. We were much gratified in witnessing the pleasure evinced by the inmates when they saw us, of whom they had heard. Even the smallest urchin in the orphan asylums of that distant land knew the name of General Tom Thumb and to our surprise were well informed as to our relationship and movements. On one occasion when the children were assembled before us, Mr. Bleeker, to test their knowledge, asked them whether the little people they looked upon were men and women or children like themselves. They replied almost in one voice, "It's Tom Thumb and his wife, Commodore Nutt and little Minnie Warren." One little urchin about five years old, to give greater emphasis to his knowledge and judgement, shouted, "General Tom Thumb got married to Lavinia Warren by Barnum. That's Tom Thumb" (pointing) "and he's a man 'cause he's got whiskers, and that's his wife" (pointing) "and she's a woman 'cause she wears a big chignon." That boy, we concluded, had a "good head."

From Ballarat we returned to Melbourne and sailed in the steamship *Tamar* for Launceston, Van Dieman's Land (or Tasmania, as it is called), and arrived there May 26th. The census had just been taken and the population of the entire country was 99,000. The circumstance of the island being situated at the southern end of the globe reverses the seasons in relation to ours. June, July and August are the winter months, and December, January and February the summer months. It took me some little time to get used to this topsy-turvy condition of the almanac, but somehow it seemed to be in harmony with the queer things and ways of the whole country. The mountains, which mostly bear Scottish and English names, are some of them 4,500 feet high and range from that down to 1,000 feet. We traversed the island in our coaches, stopping at all towns within reach without regard to population or position, for we found ourselves objects of much attention and interest everywhere and money came in in plenty. At Oatlands—and it seemed fitting the name—we cleared out and performed in a stable, there being no hall or available place. The stable belonged to the inn where we stayed. We used the grain room as a dressing room, brushing the grain back to make space, and as we moved about a fringe of wheat and oats made a fitting finish to our skirts and bedecked our trains.

During our coach trip through this almost unknown country we had many odd experiences. One I remember particularly was a source of merriment to the whole party for many days. We had travelled all day and about five o'clock arrived at a small "station" where we were to spend the night. The proprietor greeted us cheerily and comforted us greatly by the announcement that he should give us an "American supper." We were in just the condition to appreciate this and exchanged congratulatory glances. Supper was served and we were invited to regale ourselves on boiled "punkin" and boiled salt pork. Half starved and tired as we were, the situation was irresistably [*sic*] funny, and for years after an allusion to an "American supper" would be greeted with peals of laughter.

As the "station" contained only three rooms and one bed, the matter of disposing of our party for the night became a serious problem. Mr. and Mrs. Bleeker were given the bed. The General and myself occupied the sofa, our length—or should I say the lack of it—enabling us to stretch out comfortably feet to feet. Minnie was bestowed in the cradle, from which she persistently sung "Rock Me to Sleep, Mother" till assured by my husband that he'd rock her to sleep if he could find a rock big enough. The pianist and the Commodore secured the dining table, and the rest arranged themselves as comfortably as they might, tired enough to rest almost anywhere.

At another place, after a journey of over thirty miles, we found ourselves the guest[s] of an old Scotchwoman who was nearly wild as the avalanche of [*sic*] so large a party descended upon her. With the true hospitality of her nature, she gave us welcome and soon set before us a fine supper of scones and kangaroo steak. This last was given a piquant flavor from the fact that we had that day seen a giant

143

fellow who, clearing ten or fifteen feet at a bound, had passed very near us without deigning to give us a glance. We didn't "feel to" complain, however, as we had learned that their attentions to man were sometimes too marked for safety. Our sleeping accommodations here were even worse than those we had experienced before; but we were young, tired and good-natured, and our hostess kind beyond expression, so we took the soft side of stools, table and chairs and slept the sleep of youth and fatigue.

We sailed on June 27th again for Melbourne, and during the voyage we experienced a gale which for severity had never been equalled in that quarter of the globe. We were joyfully received when we landed, as from the long delay of our arrival we had been given up as lost.

There is a sandy desert intervening between the settlements in the western part of Victoria and those across the line in South Australia. As it would cause much delay in going several hundred miles to the coast and then having to wait for a passing steamer, Mr. Bleeker determined to cross the desert with our coaches. It was a perilous undertaking, but we had confidence in our manager and felt no fear. The mail was carried across once a week in a light vehicle. There were two lakes on the route—Lakes Alexandrina and Victoria—which were traversed by a little steamer built expressly to carry this small vehicle and totally inadequate to carry even one of our coaches. They were connecting lakes and were 45 miles long; consequently we had to drive around them a much greater distance. The proprietor of the vehicle that carried the mail came 20 miles to dissuade us from undertaking the journey, but Mr. Bleeker gave him a characteristic reply. "I am convinced," said he, "that I can go wherever man or horse can go, and where I go these little people will follow." As the Yankees say, "our grit was up," and we said, "Don't give it up; we'd rather sleep on the bare earth than be charged with lack of courage." We started and completed the journey in six days—over 200 miles—averaging 33 miles a day when we had been told we couldn't cover over sixteen, the horses sometimes sinking almost to their knees in the sand. The only guide we had was the sun and the track made by the small mail wagon, and this was often entirely obliterated. As we approached the settlement on the last day, we saw hundreds of kangaroo, wallabys, emus, adjutant birds, magpies and laughing jackasses.[50] The lagoons were filled with black

144

swan, wild ducks, pelicans etc., and flying overhead, flocks of cockatoos. We carried feed for the horses and sufficient food for ourselves to last. At noon we usually stopped and searched for fresh water, which was only to be found in holes dug beneath the sand by the drovers who were compelled to bring their cattle across the desert to find a market. These wells fill during the rainy season, but many of them become dry. Around them would be lying the bleached skeletons of poor beasts, no doubt killed by excessive drinking after too long a thirst. The percentage of loss in moving cattle across the country was very great, but they were lessening it yearly by furnishing stations over the route. The last day we journeyed 30 miles and reached the Murray River at 3 P.M. and were ferried across to Wellington, a miserable little village half buried in sand. After performing in ten different towns, we arrived at Adelaide August 8th. We performed in the town hall, a magnificent building, for one week; it seated 2,000 persons and was filled at every entertainment.

In going from Portland to Belfast we forded a river and had an exciting experience, as we came near being drowned. It was a dangerous undertaking and our employes expressed their fears, so Mr. Bleeker said he would not insist upon their accompanying us. I had faced many perils and was anxious to try this new excitement. We left Portland about 4 o'clock in the morning and drove 20 miles before we came to the river. It was about an eighth of a mile wide, with a strong current and evidently deep, being swollen by the rains. Our guide's actions and remarks were not very encouraging. He gazed up and down the river and hesitatingly said, "It is greatly swollen."

"Are you sure you know the ford?" inquired Mr. B.

"Positive!" replied he. "I can find it if the river is not too high."

"Then try it first," said Mr. B.

He mounted one of the horses, entered the river, disappeared down the stream under an overhanging bank, then reappeared shortly after, striking at an angle across, his horse going deeper at every step. Suddenly the animal made a plunge as if he had stepped off a ledge and began to swim. His rider turned him and regained a footing; he then progressed and reached the other side. We began to feel anxious. After resting a few moments, the rider recrossed, the horse retaining his footing although at times deeply submerged. Mr.

145

Bleeker looked at us and asked, "Now, are you afraid to venture?" "I'll go if you go," said Mrs. B. "And we'll go wherever you go," said Minnie and myself. "All right," said the General and Commodore, "we're no cowards." "We'll go," said Mr. B., and helped us into the coach. "Now mount and go ahead," said he to the guide, who did so, we following. Entering the water, we followed him down the stream, keeping close in shore until we came to a thick bush growing beneath the overhanging bank. "Turn quick and sharp!" shouted the guide to our driver. "Head straight for that cross on the other side," pointing to a small white cross on the further bank. I involuntarily thought how keeping our eyes on the cross had proved helpful in soul trials, and here the symbol was to save our bodies as well. We progressed, each moment deeper and deeper until our coach was submerged and the water covered the floor. The driver, with failing heart, pulled up. This was the deepest water over the bar. "Urge them! Urge the horses!" shouted the guide.

The driver plied his whip about the horses' heads but, half swimming, they scarce had power to move the coach. It was a critical moment. With a tremendous effort, at length they succeeded, and we slowly emerged and stood shortly after upon terra firma. The crosses were the landmarks, and it required a man with a steady nerve and a good eye to drive a four-in-hand in a direct line with the knowledge that a deviation of a few feet would be fraught with a death peril. We all remained silent during the passage—not a word or sound was uttered—although we were caged like rats in a trap with no chance of escape or rescue if we had rolled off the bar. That fact speaks well for the strength of our nerves. With light hearts we traversed the remainder of the distance, 23 miles, to Belfast.

It is unnecessary to mention the names of the towns we visited en route to Sydney. The new and magnificent town hall at Melbourne having just been completed, we gave the opening entertainment and devoted the receipts to local charities. The yield to the charities, despite a terrific rainstorm, was over $2,000.

The rainy season having commenced, we made preparations for any delay that might be caused by the floods. We left Seymour, where we had performed, in a pouring rain, and when about two miles away one of our coaches "bogged down." We had just crossed a little rivulet then about 4 inches deep; before the coach was extricated this little stream was two feet deep and rising rapidly, and we reluctantly returned to Seymour. The day of our arrival at Seymour we had observed a large boat in the yard of the hotel and wondered at its presence, as there was no stream of consequence within an area of 30 miles. Seeing the boat, Minnie playfully said, "Give me a boat ride?" The landlord looked down at her rather gravely as he replied, "My little lady, we may have to use that boat before you leave, and it may be the means of saving many lives." His words were verified. All the night of our return he was busy with efforts to assist those in peril, bringing in the distressed ones until the hotel was filled with women and children. The next morning revealed a submerged town. There were but three buildings which had escaped inundation: the hotel, the bank and a flouring mill. These contained all of the inhabitants except such as had escaped to the hills at the first rising of the water. I shall never forget that night. From our windows we peered into the darkness, watching the torches as they were waved from the different houses. The cries for help upon all sides mingled with the rushing and roaring of the waters from the hills. These sounds, accompanied by the bellowing of cattle, bleating of sheep and howling of dogs, made a fearful chorus. We remained in Seymour for five days before the water had sufficiently abated for us to depart.

When the flood came there was a depressing sense of helplessness at the ceaseless rise of water. Nothing to do, no power to resist, only to wait the silent, relentless coming up higher and higher on the sticks set to mark it and see it slowly burying rail by rail the unavailing fences. In the stable the horses were slung to lift them above the inundated floor and our ponies were coaxed and dragged into the loft. A solitary goat bleated forlornly from the door of the mill till a kind-hearted stableboy bore him to high ground, where he calmly ignored the flood and regaled himself on the branches of immersed trees.

We opened at Sydney October 4th and performed a season of three weeks with immense success, after which we proceeded to the north, visiting a large number of towns. While at Sydney, His Royal Highness the Duke of Edinburgh (second son of Queen Victoria) visited us several times at the hotel. The evening before our departure he honored us with his company to supper; his equerry Sir Elliot Yorke accompanied him and they remained with us until the "wee sma' hours." He complimented us with the remark that he had experienced an evening's enjoyment rarely received by him. Minnie's triumphs began when the Duke invited her to the ball given in his honor by the Governor-General. Minnie looked on it as a joke and accepted in high glee, going in costume as Little Red Riding Hood, while Commodore Nut[t] went as Dandy Pat, a character less widely known but popular at that time. The two excited much attention—so much, especially after the Duke had danced several times with Minnie, that he carefully escorted [her] to the royal box to secure her from intrusion. She excited much envy and some jealousy, but with the impulsive independence of her Yankee birthright she ignored it all and danced and flirted with the Duke to his great delight. I tried to subdue her a little, but it was no use. She saw her opportunity and made the most of it, laughing to scorn the chidings of "old married people." She and the Duke became great friends, and when on one occasion he found her making lemonade at some gathering, he avowed his intention of having some of that lemonade though it invariably hurt him. To which Minnie laughingly replied it would be quite in keeping with her republican principles to "knock out" a possible king. Minnie's aptitude for slang was a source of constant anxiety to Mrs. Bleeker and myself. The crumbs of royal attention which fell to my share were only to act as Minnie's chaperon and occasionally to sing while the Duke played my accompaniaments [sic].

During a period of nine months while in Australia, we traversed a distance of five thousand three hundred miles overland (nearly the entire distance by coach) and performed in one hundred and five different cities and towns.

Chapter 18

ARRIVAL AT MADRAS, B. INDIA. OVERLAND 3,500 MILES.
BANGALORE. A NAUTCH DANCE. CALCUTTA, JUMALPORE,
BENARES. THE MONKEY TEMPLE. GOLDEN TEMPLE. KING OF
BENARES PRESENTS AN ELEPHANT. ALLAHABAD, THE MOST
SACRED PLACE ON EARTH. THE PILGRIMS' CAMP. CAWNPORE,
LUCKNOW, DELHI. THE JUMMA MUSJID. RELICS OF
MAHOMET. A HAIR FROM MAHOMET'S BEARD. MEERUT, UM-
BALLA, LAHORE, AGRA. "THE TAJ." JUBBALPORE. BOMBAY.

ON SATURDAY, NOVEMBER 5TH, we left Sydney in the same steamer, the *Malta*, that conveyed us to the Colonies. On the 7th we landed at Melbourne and attended a ball given in honor of "the little people." We again sailed on the following day and arrived at Point du Galle on the 28th. On the 30th we sailed in the P. & O. steamship *Surat* for Madras, which place we reached December 3d. There is no harbor, vessels casting anchor in an open roadstead. Passengers are landed in boats called "masulahs," made of planks sewed together with cocoanut fiber or coir. The smaller kinds consist of three cocoanut logs lashed together forming a raft called a "catamaran." The masulahs are light and well calculated to live in the tremendous surf which prevails all along the coast.

149

An enormous tent formed of the leaves of the pendal tree had been built by a company of Portugese [*sic*] for circus performances. We procured it, and as it required a week to make it available for our use, we immediately went to Bangalore, 216 miles inland in the province of Mysore, and performed 3 days. Returning to Madras, we gave our performances to large audiences of Europeans and wealthy natives. On the 14th we received a visit from His Royal Highness the Maharajah of Vizianagram and suite, he having previously signified his intention of calling. He was dressed in French military costume, but wore a close-fitting cap embroidered with gold and sparkling with jewels. After a pleasant interview he departed, leaving with us a souvenir of his visit.

Among our callers was a Roman Catholic priest who possessed the complexion and characteristic features of a native, and whom we received as such. Our surprise was almost consternation when he spoke, to hear a rich brogue that would have done credit to Tipperary. Minnie couldn't master her wonder, but stood and gazed at his dark face and hands, while he talked to the General with that unmistakable Irish brogue, as if she could not solve the riddle. We are accustomed to the effects of intermarriages as developing in complexion or feature, but here was a case where the mixture of blood found no expression save in the tongue; and from our American knowledge of the antagonism between Irishmen and "nagurs," the effect of [this] pronounced Irish brogue from the lips of a black man was startling.

A deputation of native baboos or wealthy merchants waited upon our manager, introduced by Sundahram, our native landlord, who acted as interpreter. The Hindoo wives of the higher caste are never allowed to be seen by or come face to face with any of the male sex except their husbands and the immediate members of their household. Sundahram had never seen his sister-in-law after her marriage. The deputation stated that they desired to have a space allotted to them in the tent where they could suspend blinds through which their wives could see without being seen. They had previously invited us to their residences, but we could not accept the invitation as it would require too much time. The privilege was granted them and the next morning a bevy of servants came and suspended the blinds. In the evening about 50 of the ladies arrived at the private entrance to the tent and were ushered to their seats; their

150

faces were entirely covered with the exception of one eye. They were all barefooted, with the toes filled with rings of gold and silver. The space allotted them was directly beside the stage and so masked in that they could have a clear sight. When they removed the covering which enveloped their figures, their rich costumes were displayed. Their arms were bare to the shoulder and encircled with gold armlets set with precious stones. Many of them possessed fine features; their bright black eyes gave animation to their countenances, and had it not been for their sooty complexions they would have been decidedly handsome. After the performance they retired by the way of my dressing room, stopping to greet Minnie and myself.

We received an invitation from a wealthy native merchant to be present at his residence on the occasion of the celebration of the first anniversary of his grandson's birthday. Coupled with the invitation was the information that the most celebrated nautch girls would be present. At 11 P.M. we went to his residence three miles from the city. Passing through an avenue of rare plants, we alighted at the centre of a long piazza. This piazza was covered with rich rugs so arranged as to leave an avenue a yard wide the entire length. At one end stood a band with tom-toms, small "jals" or gongs and an instrument resembling a guitar. We were welcomed by the host, a fine-looking portly man in rich Oriental costume. Two magnificent diamonds sparkled in his ears and his fingers were covered with jewels. There were a dozen European ladies and gentlemen (residents of Madras) present. A servant presented each of us with a nosegay; a second brought refreshments. The host at intervals approached and sprinkled us from a gold vessel with perfumed water. We were introduced to a number of his distinguished guests: Prince Oomduth-ood-Dowlah-Kahn-Bahadvor, His Highness the Prince of Arcot, His Highness Corela Vurniah, brother of the Maharajah of Travancore who was also present, His Highness Wudayer-Reve-Nabee-yah-Jung, Maharajah of Mysore, etc. etc. It is needless to say that we bowed without attempting the names.

Presently the music played and a nautch girl advanced into the avenue and commenced her peculiar but graceful movements. She was a star in her profession, receiving two hundred rupees for her service which she expended almost entirely in procuring jewels to adorn her person. Her costume certainly astonished us. Upon her

151

head she wore a circular crowned cap of gold tissue in which diamonds, rubies, sapphires and pearls were ingeniously and thickly placed. Her hair was braided and fell in thick plaits down her back, the ends fringed with gold thread upon which were strung beads of Oriental pearls. The upper part of her person was covered with a waist of blue silk fitting tight to the body, over which was a crimson cloth jacket such as now would be called an Eton jacket and from which the present style is modeled—both waist and jacket heavily embroidered with gold thread. From her waist hung a blue silk skirt reaching to the knee, embroidered in stripes representing a running vine; beneath was a pair of Turkish trowsers of gold tissue. Her ankles were encircled with silver bells, and upon her feet were Oriental slippers with a large emerald surrounded by brilliants upon each instep. Her arms were naked to the shoulder with a broad armlet set with jewels above each elbow. In her left nostril was a gold hoop of such diameter that it reached to the chin; a broad crescent upon the hoop was set with diamonds, rubies and emeralds. Long jeweled pendants hung from her ears, and drooping across her forehead and temples [was] a golden fringe strung with pearls. Her waist was encircled with a broad gold band with a cluster of emeralds and diamonds in the centre. Upon every finger she wore one or more jewels. Her age, I was told, was 16. Advancing with a step similar to the "minuet de la cour," the bells tinkling at every movement, she stopped at every 3 or 4 steps, twisted her arms and body, and rolling her eyes expressing [sic] in pantomime the passions of love, anger, fear, sorrow etc.—the actions combined forming a little romance. Altogether it was a remarkable scene and a remarkable performer.

After the infant in whose honor the festivities were given had been exhibited to us, the host led us to his wife's apartments, where we were introduced to a large noble-looking woman, a fitting companion for her husband. She received us with great kindness and with every evidence of pleasure. We returned to the city at one o'clock A.M.

It was at Madras that I did my first sleepwalking and, for the matter of that, my last too, I think. The general appearance of insecurity in the houses, the separating screens not reaching the ceiling, the presence of hosts of natives and their close watch upon our every movement, the novelty and perhaps fatigue all combined to make me excessively nervous, and in a moment of half-sleep I

152

dreamed that someone had stolen the General's diamond ring. In the same half-sleep I said to him, "Charlie, give me your ring." He did so, and with the unreasoning cunning of a sonnambulist [*sic*] I secreted it in my own clothing. My subsequent sound sleep drove all memory of the transaction from my mind, and when while at breakfast my husband asked for the ring, I stoutly denied all knowledge of it. Our consequent excitement attracted the attention of the proprietor who, calling his servants, announced to them the loss, with the further statement that unless it was found they would be beheaded. The poor fellows looked so distressed that it almost broke my heart, and the anxiety I felt brought on an hysterical condition which did not tend to lessen the excitement. Meantime, the General endeavored to recall to my mind details of which he claimed he was perfectly cognizant. I was driven nearly wild with the entreaties and upbraidings of them all, added to the sense of responsibility for the lives of the trembling servants constantly protesting their innocence. At last, in sheer desperation I drove everybody from the room and sat down in silence to think it out. I was successful. I recalled the dream and the action which seemed a part of it, and went and brought out the ring. The landlord was as pleased as I, and the terrified servants rallied promptly from their dismay under the influence of a liberal bestowal of "buckshees[h]."

On the 17th [of] December we embarked on the P. and O. steamship *Mooltan* and arrived at Calcutta on the 21st. We stopped at the Great Eastern Hotel and gave our entertainments in the city hall. The late lamented Lord Mayo, Viceroy of India, and family entertained and appeared to take great interest in us.

We remained in Calcutta until the 8th of January 1871, when we started upon our overland journey to Bombay. Our first stopping place was Jumalpore, 300 miles from Calcutta. It lies at the foot of [the] Monghyr Hills. In the town are extensive locomotive works employing over 500 Europeans, for whose families the manufacturers have erected neat and substantial dwellings, laid out streets and squares and formed a municipal government, the original native village being embraced within its precinct. The hills abound in tigers, hyenas and jackals; the jackals were prowling around our bungalow all night, sniffing at our windows and "making night hideous" with their bark. A fortnight before we arrived a tiger was killed on the outskirts of the town, and a month previous an Englishman and his wife were walking within the limits of the town and a native milkman was upon the opposite side, when to their horror they saw a large tiger spring from the bushes beside the road, seize the native and carry him off to the hills. It is not difficult to imagine the effect of such a tale on us, especially as, no vehicle being obtainable, we were compelled to walk to and from the hall at night. I know I mentally vowed that if I ever got back to dear old New England I'd know enough to stay there. But once safely away from their vicinity, tigers and frights both faded from the picture, and later travels were not hampered by recollections.

From Jumalpore we went to the "Sacred City," Benares. This "holy city" is situated on the Ganges, which is here about six hundred yards wide. It is built in the form of a crescent on a cliff eighty feet high, which is necessary, too, as these inconstant rivers have a trick of rising from thirty to fifty feet and inundating everything which that depth can cover. But these cliffs give opportunity for those beautiful flights of marble steps called "ghats" leading down to the water.

The city is very ancient. We were too fresh from our school books to take humbly the statement that Benares was centuries old when Christ was born and had been a seat of learning eons before Plato taught. It was originally called Kshatra, a name derived from the first rajah who reigned there, it is supposed, 1600 years before Christ. According to that the city might be regarded as small of its age! Within the city limits are over one thousand temples to native gods and several Mahomedan [sic] mosques. It was here Buddha spoke 2,500 years ago, and if that tooth said to be his fitted his mouth, it must have been capable of big words. So "holy" is Benares, anyone who has even been there is considered sacred and cleansed from the faults of ordinary mortals. I trust this will be remembered by my friends!

Two of the temples are quite celebrated. The first, called Doorga Khond, is also known as the "Monkey Temple," a lofty pyramidal building, the lines being broken by numerous turrets with elaborately carved figures of animals sacred in Hindoo mythology. The great peculiarity here is the enormous number of monkeys disporting themselves in and around the building. There are thousands of them, for as no one dares to kill one and they are a long-lived creature, the number rapidly increases. We purchased a quantity of koee (a native grain) [and] gave it to the priest, who scattered it on the pavement and then giving a peculiar cry, we were surrounded by hundreds of the absurd creatures in a few seconds. Some of them were larger than myself. We gave the priest "bucksheesh" and departed, glad to escape the noise.

A mile from the "Monkey Temple" and located in the most crowded part of the city is the "Golden Temple." It is dedicated to Shiva and consists of three rooms raised upon a stone platform and crowned with three domes, two of which are overlaid with gold. No one is allowed to enter the inner temple, the doors of which are of silver, where the hideous figure is enshrined; but we somehow seemed to be held as exceptions to all rules and were allowed within the portals. The god is a large stone idol, closely resembling the pictures of it in our school books. Together with a number of smaller idols, before all of which devotees were worshipping, there were about thirty sacred bulls and cows, with garlands of flowers around their necks, quietly feeding, attended by priests. With the crowd of unclean worshippers, the drenched floors and the filth of the animals, it was far from a desirable place. It is said—and we saw it done—that kissing the tail of one of these sacred cows is a preventive of hunger. Taking into consideration the accompanying sights and odors, I've no doubt of the efficacy of the charm. I lost my appetite without resorting to the "holy" ceremony.

I have almost forgotten to mention that while in Benares the King of Benares visited us; he was a very benevolent-looking old gentleman. He urged us to visit his palace 7 miles distant from the city, but we could not spare the time. Early the next morning, after his visit, we were surprised by the appearance at our bungalow of two enormous elephants, one of them the largest I ever saw. The old King had a herd of sixty and sent two for our use. The largest was his favorite tiger-hunting elephant, the King being very fond of hunting. They were covered with trappings and had howdahs upon their backs. We rode on the large one while we remained. The smaller one he wished to present to us, "mahout" and all, but we felt obliged to refuse the present. The royal old gentleman evidently did not recognize the difficulties that might accrue to our travelling party were we to take an elephant on our hands.

After leaving Benares we stopped at several places before reaching Allahabad, where we crossed the river Jumna upon a bridge 3,224 feet long. Allahabad is also called a "sacred city" and is supremely holy, being built at the junction of three rivers—the Ganges, the Jumna and a third which exists only in the imagination of the natives, being nowhere visible to the naked eye. But as it is supposed to flow from the mouth of Brahma and to eventually return to it, dead bodies, even of animals, are thrown into it and left to float down on its current as a sure means of arriving ultimately in the Hindoo heaven. The General hoped "Brahma had a filter in his throat," which from our irreligious point of view did seem desirable.

Somehow there's something attractive in this unquestioning belief that even animals may possess immortality. One wouldn't be sorry to meet a faithful dog in the golden streets, knowing that his unpurchasable integrity deserved more than this world could give him.

The city was swarming with pilgrims, for Allahabad is the Mecca of the Hindoos, and during the months of January and February at least a million pilgrims from all parts of India take their way on foot to bathe in and carry away with them some of the sacred water. Along the road for miles we saw thousands of these pilgrims wending their way to the sacred spot, or having completed the pilgrimage were returning, carrying jars filled with the water. All looked worn and emaciated, having traveled perhaps a thousand miles and still having to traverse the same distance to reach their homes. What a powerful faith it must be to sustain them in these trials and hardships! When a pilgrim arrives at the bank of the river, he sits down and has his head shaved, allowing the hairs to fall into the stream, the sacred writings promising him one million years' residence in paradise for every hair thus deposited (bald-headed men should take notice). After being shaved, he bathes. The native barbers reap a rich harvest. Their charge for shaving is one rupee (fifty cents); at any other time and place their fee is only one penny, English.

Before going upon the sacred ground we viewed the scene from the fortifications; the next day we went through the vast camp. It was a gay sight and resembled an enormous fair. We next visited the Kooshroo Gardens. They are entered through a noble gateway 60 feet high and 50 feet deep. Kooshroo was Akbar's grandson. I ascended to the roof of the sultan's mausoleum.

There was an insect in India which I have never forgotten. I can't tell its name, being in the position so many find themselves when they say "I remember your face, but I can't call your name." That's precisely my condition when I think of this long-legged insect, which Minnie, true to her Yankee instincts, called a "critter." I remember his face perfectly, but I can't call his name. I was introduced to him more than once, or perhaps I should say he introduced himself. He seemed to me only a huge pea-green grasshopper, and I was assured he was harmless. But it was the unexpectedness of him to which I objected. His arrivals and departures were unannounced and there was a jerky uncertainty to his movements, eminently disconcerting. Lizards too had a way of slipping about so silently that your first intimation of their presence was when you laid your hand on the cold slimy thing[s]. They say one gets used to them, but I've a firm belief I should go with the Frenchman's horse in the process.

From Allahabad we went to Cawnpore. It is here that the most diabolical atrocities of the mutiny of 1857 were committed.

[The next several leaves of the manuscript are taken up with the history of the Indian Mutiny and descriptions of places and memorials associated with it. After leaving Cawnpore the party traveled to Lucknow, where they toured the Martinière, saw the sights associated with the relief of that city, and performed in a theatre fitted up in a part of the harem formerly belonging to Nuseer-ood-deen Hyder.]

We returned to Cawnpore to remain overnight. While seated at supper we heard a terrible outcry—dogs barking, women screaming and a general hubbub. Rushing out to ascertain the cause, we saw a bright light as if the place were in flames, but soon ascertained that the jackals had made a raid upon the native village and they were driving them off by building fires and setting the dogs upon them. However interesting jackals may be as a study in natural history, we felt that as neighbors they were not without disadvantages.

From Cawnpore we proceeded to Delhi.

157

[There follows a sketch of the city of Delhi and the sights to be seen there, including the Jamma Masjid; several surprising relics of Mohammed, among them a solitary hair of the Prophet's beard, which Lavinia scrutinized; and the tomb of the poet Khusroo, author of The Arabian Nights. The troupe then progressed to Meerut, Umballa, and Lahore, with the atrocities of the late Mutiny still occupying their minds.]

As we journeyed we heard constant reports of another anticipated outbreak, and troops were moving daily from point to point. The day we arrived at Lahore, lying in the Punjab, we found the few Europeans in great excitement in anticipation of an uprising at midnight. A regiment of English soldiers arrived the same afternoon, which, if an outbreak was really intended, stopped it. Of course we all felt anxious. From Lahore we returned and stopped at Agra, formerly called Akbarabad, the city of the great Akbar. The principal objects of interest are the fort and the Taj.

[These two objects are also dutifully described.]

From Agra we returned to Allahabad, thence to Jubbalpore. The scenery was very fine. We saw plenty of game: spotted deer, antelope, pea-fowl, partridge. The jungles near the road abound in tigers, leopards, hyena[s] etc. The knowledge of this fact served to tone down our enthusiasm at the unusual scenes and prevented any undue hilarity by the way. Elephants too were said to be plenty, but as we had made the acquaintance of several tame ones and had no pressing desire to "meet up" with a wild one, we kept strictly to the roadway, stopping occasionally at a town till we reached Bombay, a distance of 850 miles from Allahabad. In Bombay we were told there is probably no place on earth with such a motley population. I'm ready to believe that, and also that each separate specimen used a different style of vehicle.

We traveled over three thousand five hundred miles overland in the country. I should not desire to live in British India. Servant hire is cheap: 5 or 6 rupees ($3) a month and they find [for] themselves. Every person has at least one; a family 15 or 20. We always had 8 or 10. Perhaps there may be some excuse for being lazy owing to the enervating nature of the climate. We traversed the country in the coolest and most favorable time.

Chapter 19

ARRIVAL AT ADEN. ARABIA. ISLAND SUPPOSED TO BE THE
SPOT WHERE CAIN KILLED ABEL. VOYAGE THROUGH THE RED
SEA TO EGYPT. MOUNT SINAI. VIEW OF MOCHA, JIDDAH,
YAMBO-EL-BAHR. PHARAOH'S BAY, THE SPOT WHERE
PHARAOH AND HIS HOST WERE DROWNED. SUEZ. GRAND
CAIRO. ALEXANDRIA. POMPEY'S PILLAR.

ON SATURDAY, FEB. 18TH, 1871, we sailed in [the] steamship *Surat*
and arrived at Aden on the 25th. Aden, situated on the southeast
coast of Arabia, is 110 miles east of the entrance to the Red Sea.
There are few places so cheerless. The promontory forms a high
rocky eminence 1,800 feet above the level of the sea. It was purchased from the Arabs by the English government in 1830. The
town is built upon the southeast side in a deep hollow, the crater of
an extinct volcano, and there's not a tree or blade of grass visible. The
native population is 50,000, but the whites are only 300 or 400 in
number, except the garrison of English troops. During our sojourn
ashore we were beset continually by the natives, who offered the
finest ostrich feathers for sale.

160

Leaving Aden, our course lay through the Straits of Babel
Mendeb (the "Gate of Tears"), seventeen miles in width, and thence

into the Red Sea, passing in view an island which is pointed out as the spot where Cain killed Abel. As to the truth of the assertion, it is very certain I cannot say, but from the modern standpoint anything that shortened life on that barren spot might be counted as "justifiable homicide."

One of the conundrums of my childhood was a question as to why *black*berries were red when they were green; and I thought of that when I looked into the blue depths of the Red Sea, which shades into green near the shores. But my sense of color was satisfied later on when I saw that there were patches, from a few yards to several miles in extent, of a blood-red animalculae floating on the surface, and [I] understood then how the name was given. These patches lie inside the coral reefs which guard most of the length of coast.

Next, Mocha! But there was nothing in the glaring white-washed houses to suggest the birthplace of our breakfast beverage, which later knowledge assures me is shipped from Brazil to Aden to be returned to us as "Mocha." Stretching north along the coast is the arid and burning Tehama, backed by high mountains. One of the most picturesque scenes we saw was a number of Arabs mounted upon camels approaching the city. We next passed Jiddah, the port of Mecca. Mecca, the "mother of towns," lies 60 miles eastward. Next, northward of Jiddah, lies Yambo-el-Bahr, the port of Medina. Yambo is one of the gates of the Holy City. It lies in the caravan road from Cairo to Mecca. Next come a succession of smaller ports. At its northern extremity the Red Sea is divided into two gulfs called Suez and Akaba, deriving their names from the town of Suez and the fortress of Akaba belonging to the Pasha of Egypt. Akaba serves also as a station for the caravans of pilgrims from Egypt and northern Africa. The peninsula included between the gulfs is rugged, mountainous and perfectly sterile and is called the Sinai Peninsula. It was the summit of one of these mountains that witnessed the delivery of the "Law of Moses." By the aid of telescopes we saw the sacred mount, its top partly veiled by thin light clouds. Immediately at the foot of Jabel Katrin, 8600 feet high, adjoining Jabel Mousa, the sacred mount 7,500 feet high, stands the celebrated Convent of St. Catherine. The whole of the peninsula is inhabited by Bedouins or wandering Arabs.

161

Between Toor and Suez we crossed Pharaoh's Bay (Birket Faroun). Tradition names this as the place where Pharaoh's hosts were overwhelmed by the sea. The gulf is very narrow and rough owing to the tides and many countercurrents, their action increased by the winds from the rocky clefts of the mountains upon both sides. There is a legend that on the anniversary of the destruction of the Egyptians a phantom army—horses, chariots and soldiers—may be seen struggling in the water. We didn't meet them!

We arrived at Suez on the 4th of March. The population embraces Europeans, Persians, Turks, Moors, Algerines and Egyptians, and their various methods of showing surprise, admiration or approval was a matter of great interest to me. The town of Suez has little to recommend it to memory and would have small place in history but for its now being the port of the ship canal. It has a few European hotels, well kept, and to the stranger one point of interest is the ancient defenses, built to keep out the Bedouins of the Sinai Peninsula but, no longer needed, now in ruins. When De Lesseps is immortalized for his great work on this continent-severing canal, let it be remembered that portions of it were completed eons before his birth.

Over a branch of the Alexandrian Railroad we went to Al Kahira or Grand Cairo. The city is surrounded by walls, outside of which are beautiful gardens of palm trees. The streets are narrow, often only ten or twelve feet wide, and many of them still more confined in appearance by the projecting stone copings and overhanging windows of fretted stone and carved wood. On all sides are open arches. As a relief to the narrow streets [there] are many large squares; the finest, the Esbekijeb, lies in the center of the city. Upon the western bank of the Nile is the village of Ghizah, where the necessary conveyance—a donkey generally—may be obtained for a visit to the Pyramids. To us the donkey ride was an irresistable [*sic*] attraction, and mounting mine I was amused at the look of shrewd wonder he turned back at me. Evidently my weight did not quite fulfil his expectations, but as he expressed no disapproval and trotted off as if eager to escape further burden, I had no desire to find fault. Each of our company was soon mounted, and our cavalcade elicited shouts of merriment from staring Arabs as well as from ourselves.

162

The Pyramids were very interesting to me, but I cannot hope to describe them any better than hundreds have done before me [and] therefore shall not attempt it. The Commodore, like a true Yankee, seemed to be oppressed with a sense of unnecessary expenditure and said he expected to lie still when he was dead, "without all that mess of stone on top" of him.

The wonderful grandeur of the Pyramids must be the same today, but now that trolley cars take globe-trotters to them, all the fun is eliminated from the process of getting there and much of the novelty. I care nothing to go now, but prefer to remember them as they impressed me then, set in the framework of crude methods of locomotion and haloed about with the enthusiasm of youthful enjoyment. For whatever they were intended, the mystery now is how could such wondrous single pieces have been quarried, transported and put in place. We have a fashion of believing that little is beyond the engineering resources of our day, but two thousand three hundred years ago some mind that lacked the results of our boasted civilization planned and executed engineering feats before which we stand in awe.

Cairo interested me particularly because of the great variety in its population, like many other places in that vicinity. Its census at that time gave 120,000, including Egyptians, Arabs, Jews, Turks, Persians, French, Italians and English—in fact, every nation is represented. I had almost neglected to mention that the late Khedive—he was then in power and was absent when we reached Egypt—upon his return offered us the use of his own special train and quarters in his palace at Grand Cairo and a present of £500 sterling ($2,500) for two days' entertainments; but it was too late, as our time was then limited on account of the sailing of the steamer from Alexandria.

Two thousand years ago Alexandria was among the largest cities of the world and distinctively Egyptian. Now, in its cosmopolitan changes, one scarce realizes the mysterious antiquity of this land of the lotus. The principal street in the Frank quarter has large handsome shops, hotels, restaurants, reading rooms etc., and American merchants were well represented. This portion of the city was destroyed by the bombardment of the English during their trouble with the Egyptians since we were there, but there are many traces of antiquity to recall the twenty centuries' age of this now modernized city. The large towers flanking the old wall are quite perfect. The front portico and a few porphyry pillars of Caesar's palace remain. Cleopatra's palace was built upon the wall facing the port; not far from the site of the palace were the two obelisks called

Cleopatra's needles. We little expected to see one of them afterwards standing in Central Park, New York City. The other is in London.

Upon the other side of the city and serving as a landmark for ships stands the majestic Pompey's Pillar. The upper member of the base and the shaft are of one single piece of pink granite eighty-six feet long and twenty-seven feet in circumference; the Corinthian capital is nine feet high; the entire height, including the base, one hundred and fourteen feet.

Minnie and I took a ride in a vehicle which appealed to us by its novelty. It was two-wheeled, without cover, drawn by a donkey; and the driver was a typical native. He resembled an animated rag-bag. Perhaps the term "animated" may express too much. It means in this case simply that the man was not dead. The accommodations for sitting were merely more rags that differed from his only in the fact that they had no body within them. The whole arrangement was so comically original that we insisted on riding, though under strong protest from the rest of the party. I do not remember the name of the vehicle or its driver, but eternity will not serve for me to forget the odor. We went to the Delta to see the pilgrims on their way to Mecca. Seeing many of them with water bottles on their heads carried my thought back to my Sunday school days. As I pored over the queer pictures in my lesson book, I little dreamed I should ever see the reality and, standing in Egypt, look across to Arabian shores.

Chapter 20

Across the Mediterranean to Brindisi. Across the Continent appearing before King Victor Emmanuel, Emperor Francis Joseph and royalty everywhere. Another tour of Great Britain. Return to U.S. June 22d, 1872. Tour of the U.S. Escape from the Newhall House, Milwaukee, Jan 10th, 1883, during its conflagration. Death of Mrs. Bleeker, one of the victims, 12 days after. Death of Gen. Tom Thumb.

We sailed from Alexandria March 11th and landed at Brindisi, Italy, on the 14th March 1871. A description of the Continental cities would be superfluous. Suffice it to say we visited Naples, seeing Vesuvius in its angry mood, vomiting forth smoke, flame and immense rocks; walked the silent streets of Pompeii; looked in at Herculaneum; went to Rome; mounted to the highest seat in the ruined Coliseum; visited the ancient Catacombs, St. Peter's, the Vatican, St. John's Lateran; and stood within its ancient cloisters upon and beneath the two marble stones which it is averred were made to measure the height of our Saviour. "Myriads," said the verger, "have been guaged [sic] by that standard, yet no man has been found to measure the exact height." We mounted the identical steps

165

our Redeemer ascended (so it is claimed) and passed through the same portals He entered belonging to Pontius Pilate's house and which were removed to Rome during the reign of one of the early popes. We stood in the Pantheon, the Forum; sailed upon the Grand Canal in Venice; attended service at St. Mark's; visited the Doge's palace; put our hands in the Lion's mouth; stood in the trial chamber of the Inquisition; ascended the steps and entered the "Hall of Torture"; descended and followed the footsteps of the victims across the Bridge of Sighs, down into the horrible dungeons dark and foul. We crossed the Rialto; attended the solemn services upon Good Friday in the grand cathedral of Milan. We were received by King Victor Em[m]anuel at his palace in Florence; also by Prince Humbert, the late king, and Marguerite, his beautiful wife. In Vienna we appeared before the Emperor Francis Joseph at his palace; and indeed we stood within most of the palaces of Europe and were received by royalty in every capital.

April 18th, 1871, we landed in England and traversed again the United Kingdom, exhibiting in 208 different cities and towns.[51] We sailed from Liverpool June 12th, 1872, in [the] steamship *Egypt* and sighted Sandy Hook on the 22d, being a period of three years and one day from the time of our departure.

To sum up the result of our tour, we traveled 55,487 miles (31,216 miles by sea) [and] gave 1,471 entertainments in 587 different cities and towns in all climates of the world, without missing through accident or illness a single performance wherever announced. For the kindness of Divine Providence in protecting us from all harm during our perilous journeys, our hearts are truly thankful.[52]

After a much needed rest we again started in September and visited all of the States and Upper and Lower California, performing to immense audiences, our great three years' tour being everywhere known and talked about. In 1876 Mr. Barnum invited us to visit him at Bridgeport. After dinner he asked us into his library, as he wished to have a private conversation with us. After a little chat he said, "I feel that I am of no more use to you than the fifth wheel to a coach"; then turning to Mr. Bleeker continued, "Although I am part owner, you have been the captain of the ship so long, and I not rendering any assistance even in the working of the vessel, that I feel as if I had no right to my share of the profit from the voyages. I therefore resign my interest, which you may take and divide between [the] General, Lavinia and yourself. If at any time necessities should arise whereby you may require my assistance, call upon me and I will freely aid you. I have long thought of doing this." We all thanked him heartily. "But," he continued, "don't thank me; you could easily have thrown the old man overboard long ago as thousands would have done, but I honor you for your friendship and fidelity to me. God bless you for it." And the tears stood in his eyes as he took our hands.

[The following story of an attempted robbery was written while Lavinia was revising her manuscript and is indicated as coming somewhat later in the narrative. In view of the reference to her sister Minnie, however, it would appear to be more appropriate at this point.]

At a certain hotel in New York we occupied a front room with an alcove. The peculiar arrangement of the halls was such that a passageway to Minnie's room led past both our rooms and hers and then terminated, so that any steps approaching announced that someone was coming to our rooms, as there was nothing beyond. A small window in the alcove opened something like a transom, and this window I was always careful should be locked before I went to bed. The General was always exceedingly careless of money or jewels. I never quite decided whether it was because he'd always had someone to look out for him or whether it was an inherent quality of the masculine mind. Later experiences incline me to the latter opinion. One night he made me especially nervous by bringing home a large quantity of money. Added to that he had lugged in, in his own hands, several cases of paste diamonds which he thought it expedient for me to wear in place of my real ones. I begged him to put them downstairs in the safe or anywhere to get them out of the room. But he persisted in saying everything was all right and went to bed. It always seemed to me that though the General was small in stature, he had certain masculine qualities as fully developed as did my stalwart brothers, and obstinacy was not the least among them. I

167

too went to bed but not to sleep, and not until I had put the money between the mattrasses [*sic*]. As I lay shivering with a nameless terror, I was sure I saw the small window move slightly. I elbowed the General and whispered my suspicion. "O nonsense!" said he aloud, in spite of my nudging. "Don't bother." But I bothered all the same; and when a little later I saw the window cautiously opened a little way, I insisted on his waking to share my observations, if no more. Meantime I had twice heard rapid steps come down past our door and felt they indicated something wrong. At last the General was convinced my fears were not wholly groundless and he began to dress, when suddenly we heard a fearful crash in the corridor, followed by sounds of a struggle and a hurried tramp of feet. Investigation proved that thieves had entered the house, having seen the General bring in the cases of jewelry and knowing he always carried large sums of money. Peering in at our window, they may have been deceived into thinking we were children, or they may have been waiting for me to get to sleep. The footsteps I had heard were those of the porter, whose suspicions were aroused. Not finding them on that floor, he started up the next flight in pursuit, and the crash which had wakened everybody was caused by the fall of a heavy table which the robbers—there were two—dropped over the banisters intending to crush him. His escape was almost a miracle, but he did escape; and the assistance which the crash called enabled him to capture them both, and they then confessed their intention to "rob General Tom Thumb." The alarm and excitement made Minnie quite ill, but in all the consequent anxiety I found myself smiling at the story one of the boarders told me. She said she heard a slight noise and discovered a long wire with a hooked end industriously fishing at the ring of her watch as it lay on the dressing table. As she looked, the watch slowly rose from the table and proceeded to approach the transom. Too frightened to make an outcry, she seized her watch, and the uncanny hook hastily retreated. Almost immediately thereafter she heard the crash which had startled us all. To my mind the picture of that watch travelling through the air, and she rushing frantically after it, has always seemed so ludicrous, I smile even now as I write it.

168

In the summer of 1878 my sister Minnie died at our home in Middleboro. And here I will refute a general impression which meets me everywhere I go, which is that Minnie married Commodore Nutt. This impression arose, I think, from the fact that the Commodore was groomsman at the marriage of Gen. Tom Thumb and myself, and my sister officiated as bridesmaid. Then they were with us in our subsequent travels over the United States and Canada, and completed our "quartette" in our trip around the world. Minnie married Major Edward Newell, a "little man" with whom she became acquainted in New York.[53] He is now in London, England, and has a second wife. Minnie's grave is on the hillside in the beautiful cemetery of my native town.

It proved one of the greatest trials of my life to go again before the public without her, but it was the lifework marked out for me and I resumed it just as others resume their regular duties after an overwhelming grief. Even now I do not find it easy to speak of it. All my other sisters and brothers were [of] normal size, and hence she and I were in a measure isolated from them and brought nearer each other.

The General and I continued our travels with flattering success until 1881, when Mr. Barnum induced us by a most liberal offer to travel with his "Greatest Show on Earth" for that season.[54] Although every convenience and luxury was ours that such a life afforded, it was not to our liking and at the end of the season we withdrew and again resumed our usual travel.

An event happened on January 10th, 1883, the remembrance of which has ever since cast a gloom over my life and indirectly was the cause of a change in my future. I allude to the burning of the Newhall House in Milwaukee, with all its accompanying horrors. My dearly beloved Mrs. Bleeker was the only victim of our party. Although her husband rescued her from the flames, she was so badly injured that she died 12 days after. While life lasts the memory of her will ever be green in my mind.

The General never recovered from the shock of that terrible ordeal; he died suddenly from heart failure the following July.[55] I must here pause to pay a loving tribute to his memory. His excellent qualities were numerous. I never knew a person so entirely devoid of malice, jealousy or envy; he had the natural instincts of a gentleman. He was kind, affectionate and generous. He had great sympathy for children and was ever ready to do anything to make them happy. He had often remarked that he never remembered having been a child, being placed on exhibition when he was but four years of age, and was then educated to act the part of a man and put childish things away. Our married life was a happy one. I particularly emphasize this as I have frequently heard it reported that it was not congenial. He was a 33d degree Mason and was interred with the solemn and impressive rites of the Knights Templers [*sic*]. His body rests in Mountain Grove Cemetery, Bridgeport, near the remains of Mr. Barnum, with whom he had been associated during almost his entire life.[56]

After my husband's death I determined upon retiring to private life, but almost daily I received letters from managers of places of amusement in all parts of the States offering me engagements, all of which I declined. My most intimate friends urged me to forego my determination, but I refused. While visiting some friends in Bridgeport 3 months subsequent to the General's death, Mr. Barnum called upon me; and when I asked his opinion upon the subject, his reply was that I belonged to the public, and if the public wished to see me I should acquiesce. Turning to Mr. Bleeker he said, "Take her out! Take her out! If she remains as she is, her days will be shortened. You both remember when I reached the age of 62 I retired from business, under advice, for 3 years. They were years of unhappiness to me; no doubt if I had continued to be inactive I would have died. I intend when death takes me to find me in harness." He died at the age of 80, still in business. I accepted his advice and have since fulfilled many engagements with profit both to the management and myself.[57]

On Easter Monday, April 6th, 1885, I was married to Count Primo Magri at the Church of the Holy Trinity, Madison Avenue and Forty-Second Street, New York, by Reverend Mr. Watkins. As I had issued invitations only to personal friends, the large church was well filled but with no disagreeable crowding. The Count's brother, Baron Magri, acted as groomsman, and Miss Sarah Adams as bridesmaid.[58]

One bit of comedy came in of which I, of course, was not aware, but was afterward told by a friend who looked down from the gallery. When Major Newell, my sister Minnie's husband, walked up the aisle with Miss Lucy Adams, the organist, having probably no knowledge that there were other small people in the world than those he was expecting, rushed into the wedding march from *Lohengrin*. Hearing this, the officiating clergyman stepped forward and the audience rustled and craned, only to see the two, flushed and embarrassed at the unexpected attention, hurridly [*sic*] enter the first available pew. The minister wisely remained standing; the eager audience subsided to wait till the organist, sure of himself this time, filled the arches with melody; and the seemingly intermidable [*sic*] aisle was traversed by us to the glorious harmony of Mendleshon [*sic*]. In May I went with my husband to Italy, to his home at Pieva du Cinto [*Pieve di Cento*], near Bologna, and remained during the summer; and though there is everything to please the mind and eye, my love for America seemed to grow with the hours and I could not decide to make even beautiful Italy my permanent home.

An incident which may cast some doubt on whether my discretion has got the better of my valor may well be mentioned here. On our way home from Italy we were in Liverpool a few days, and one night attended the theatre to witness a play which in one scene introduced the flags of all nations. I had become so interested that I had temporarily forgotten the audience, and when "Old Glory" was brought on I sprang to the front of the box in a paroxysm of delight and yielded to the impulse to shout my joy. My confusion and embarrassment when the audience burst into sympathetic applause had best be left to the imagination of my readers.

As I am frequently interrogated concerning my husband, I will here say that both he and his brother, the Baron, are only an inch or two taller than myself. They were educated as gentlemen in Italy and have the cultivated tastes and manners to be expected of gentlemen. They are skilled in music, fencing and boxing, which latter accomplishments, however, they usually have to exercise on each other, as it isn't often they find a "fellow of their size." When not travelling, the Baron, since his wife's return to Italy, spends much of his time with the Count and myself at my brother's home in Middleboro, Massachusetts. Mr. Stratton (General Tom Thumb) built a handsome house, to which I have previously alluded, near my childhood's home and fitted it with music and billiard rooms to accommodate the miniature grand piano and the little billiard table made expressly for him as a part of our wedding outfit. After his death I broke up housekeeping and, letting my house, removed my "little" furniture to my brother's home across the way, where it now is and where I make my home in the intervals between my trips.

The Count, my husband, has "taken out his papers" and be-

171

come an American citizen. He proposes to do his duty by the country at the polls, if not up to the regulation heighth [*sic*] for army service. The Baron's taste led him to take up portraiture, and he is now an excellent crayon artist, while the Count devoted himself more exclusively to music. His taste in that direction being modeled on classic Italian methods, he has never consented to learn "catchy" songs and totally ignores "ragtime" melodies. I find myself loth to tell him that the average American taste would probably be better reached through these so-called "popular airs," and so he continues to sing his operatic selections. He plays the piano and piccalo [*sic*], his music doing much to add to our home pleasure as well as public entertainments. The Baron whistles delightfully and usually serves as accompanist to the Count's vocalization. He says his whistle "takes no room in packing" and is thus as convenient as it is agreeable.

The Baron's family consists of a wife and three children, and when his daughter married and became a mother it was said of him that he was probably the smallest grandfather in the world. His daughter died a few years since, and the Baron's wife and one of his sons are still in Italy. They were in America at one time, hence are familiar with this country and its language, but will remain there near the motherless grandchildren for a time. The younger son has recently returned here and is now in a position of trust and responsibility near Boston.

It seems as if I ought not to close without a word of my dog Topsey, who for thirteen years has been with me night and day. Latterly she has taken her part in "the cast" and has done herself as much credit on the stage as had hitherto been awarded her as a traveller. Faithful as a companion, reliable as a guard, curled in my trunk tray, quiet and observant in cars and stations, she holds a place in my heart and shall have mention in my book as a friend to be esteemed and remembered. She "went to sleep" just as I put my last words on these pages, and the two go out of my life together, their future unguessed.

When asked if I don't get tired of this public life, I am wont to answer that in a sense I belong to the public. The appearing before audiences has been my life. I've hardly known any other. It is difficult to realize that in reality I have met three generations. It is not at all unusual for people who meet me to say "I saw you years ago and have never forgotten it, and now I'm bringing my daughter that she can have it to tell of, just as I have." Not infrequently women say "Here is my grandchild! I want him to shake hands with you as his mother did when she was little." Recently I was greeted by two elderly ladies accompanied by an old gentleman, all of whom had witnessed my marriage with General Tom Thumb (Charles S. Stratton) in 1863. Then too there are many sections of [the] country where new towns have sprung up and small towns have become thriving cities. In these I am interested. Having been over the ground when it was an unbroken forest or a straggling village, the new developments are like magic to me. It is Houdon, Blitze or Herman producing live rabbits from an empty hat.[59] Also I find many old friends glad to greet me, and make new friends whom I hope to meet again. All this, taken into account with Mr. Barnum's advice—"Keep going, Mrs. Stratton, keep going! I believe if I remained inactive it would shorten my days"—has influenced me. As Mr. Barnum lived to be eighty and died in harness, I've felt he was capable of giving advice. I come of a long-lived race, most of my ancestors living to be ninety, many more than that, and one cousin of my mother's was very nearly one hundred and four when she died.

In this connection there comes to mind an incident of my second visit to Ireland, in 1872. We were to visit a place called Drogheda. Upon our arrival at the station, a porter from the hotel where we had engaged rooms met us with a note from the proprietor, stating that his wife was dying and that he had engaged accommodations for us at another inn, whither the porter conducted us. The following day the same porter conveyed us to the station in some sort of a nondescript vehicle. I asked him if the landlord's wife was dead. "Yis," said he, "God rist her sowl, she's dead!"; then added after a pause, during which our countenances assumed the proper expression of lugubrious solemnity, "'Tis thrue she's dead, but she's not dead all over yit!" I fear our faces changed expression suddenly. When I was in Boston not so many years ago, a woman who heard me introduced as Mrs. Tom Thumb stoutly asserted "Mrs. Tom Thumb is dead!" That woman must have thought she had some grounds for her assertion, but reader, like the good woman in Ireland, I'm *not dead all over yet*!

THE END

APPENDIX

Published Portions
of the Autobiography
and Additional Recollections

[*As noted in the Introduction, Lavinia wrote her autobiography with publication in mind and as early as 1901 expressed the hope to have it* put out to the public before long. *She was not destined to see her narrative in book form, but in the fall of 1906 a drastically condensed version appeared in five issues of the Sunday Magazine section of the* New York Tribune.[1] *Each of these articles, including illustrations, occupies around one and a half pages, those in the issues of 16 September, 7 October, 21 October, and 25 November skimming the manuscript, in its revised or second-draft state, from beginning to end. It would appear, however, that Lavinia was then requested to extend her recollections to an additional article, for in her fifth and final installment of 16 December—titled "Gleanings from My Autobiography: Recollections of Odd Experiences in Out of the Way Corners of the Earth during Our World Tour"—she did not keep to her announced topic but backtracked over ground previously covered, adding several anecdotes and adventures from widely scattered periods in her career. Approximately half of these are drawn directly from her autobiography, but the others are either new or else reworkings of old material, presumably written expressly to fill out the article. This additional material is here published in full.*]

175

NOTHING IN MY LONG CAREER has touched me more deeply than the souvenirs that my friends have pressed upon me. In every quarter of the globe I have received tokens of the kind regard of the many people I have met, and of these none was more curious than the elephant that the King of Benares presented to me in India.

But more embarrassing was the gift offered to me while we were at New Orleans during my first trip South with Colonel Wood before the war. One day a wealthy plantation owner came aboard our floating theater and, noticing that I paid particular attention to a beautiful mulatto girl who was with his company, he offered her to me in the politest manner possible. "You can have her, Miss Warren," he said, "if you will take her home with you." Of course, I couldn't think of becoming a slaveholder; but the poor girl used to visit me at the hotel in the firm conviction that she was my chattel.

On this trip and a later one I met many of the men who became famous afterward in the great struggle with the Confederacy. At Richmond, Jefferson Davis attended one of my receptions with his wife and daughters. He was a most chivalrous and kindly gentleman, and I have always looked back to that meeting with pleasure. General Robert E. Lee was also one of my guests at that time; and later on, at Lexington, Kentucky, I met Mrs. Lincoln, the President's wife, and her mother. We both laughed merrily when the people remarked the resemblance between us.

When we were at Wheeling, West Virginia, in 1863 we were the pets of the soldiers who were stationed in the town, and every evening the officers constituted themselves a guard to escort us with drawn sabers to the hall in which we gave our entertainments.

The turmoil of the war rendered accommodations at the hotel very uncertain, and when meal time came the officers used to go down into the kitchen to see that we at least should be well cared for. Often Commodore Nutt would go down with them to help choose the food that we preferred. Many times we had a hearty laugh when he came back to our rooms on the shoulder of one of the officers, his arms piled high with fruit and sweetmeats.

At Frankfort, Kentucky, during the same period we were terrified one evening at dinner by the announcement that Morgan, the famous guerilla leader, was coming. Great excitement prevailed, and many of the guests at the hotel were so afraid that they did not go to bed at all that night. Morgan, however, did not come, and so I missed having any real war experience.

One Sunday evening after we had returned from church Commodore Nutt, Minnie, the General, and myself were gathered in our room, when some one suggested that we pay a visit to our treasurer, whose apartment was on the same floor but around the corner in the long hall. In those days our dresses were dignified by long trains, which naturally retarded our movements somewhat; but when Minnie stepped out into the hall she challenged me with that spirit of vivacity which always characterized her, calling out, "I'm going to see how quick I can get down the hall."

She ran along, distancing even the Commodore, and soon reached the corner of the corridor which led to Mr. Bleeker's room. No sooner had she disappeared from our view than we were startled to hear her sweet little voice raise itself in fright.

"What is the matter, Minnie?" cried the General, as we redoubled our speed.

You can imagine our terror when on turning the corner we found her white as death, leaning against the wall, unable to utter a single syllable, and saw stalking down the hall a figure draped in white, with outstretched arms and staring eyes. Our cries awakened Mr. Bleeker and several of the other guests, and they opened their doors, rushing into the hall in their night clothes; but the figure had disappeared. Mr. Bleeker called up the manager of the hotel and a search was instituted, without avail.

The General insisted that we would find an explanation in the morning, and he was right, for it turned out the next day that we had met a somnambulist. The poor man was very ill with consumption and had risen from bed that night while his nurse was taking a short nap. The noise of our cries wakened him, and he was as much shocked as we were to find himself in the hall sparsely clad and surrounded by four screeching, diminutive people such as he had never before seen. In our terror I suppose we did not notice him plunge through the door into his own room, and thus we prepared the way for the mystification of the entire hotel.

That was the most uncanny experience I ever had, and although I may have been a trifle superstitious before that time, I have since held the opinion of General Tom Thumb, who always declared that he would never believe in ghosts until he could put his hand on something and find nothing there. Still, there are many queer things of this kind for which we can find no explanation.

Of all the wonder workers I have known, Mr. Barnum was easily chief. With him, as with most of the people I have met intimately, I was a veritable pet. He was continually inventing new names by which to call me, and for a long time addressed me only as "Commodore." The origin of the title was in itself amusing. It occurred while we were on a trip to New York. I had been stopping at his home in Bridgeport, where we boarded the train. At Danbury a lady entered the car and, recognizing Mr. Barnum, at once approached us.

"Why, good morning, Mrs. Knight," he said, rising. "Let me introduce you to Miss Warren."

"Oh, Mr. Barnum," she replied playfully, "you can't deceive me. I see you have Commodore Nutt dressed up as a little lady."

"But I am not trying to deceive you this time, I assure you, Mrs. Knight," he answered. "Miss Warren is really what she seems. Commodore Nutt is in New York awaiting us."

But no matter what he could say, Mrs. Knight would not be convinced. She left the train at the next station, apparently firm in the belief that I was the Commodore, and Mr. Barnum then remarked to me, "Pretty funny, Commodore, isn't it, how many people actually insist on being humbugged?"[2]

I have often said that I believed I was born for my business, and just as surely Mr. Barnum was born for his. In private or in public he was always an entertainer. He was the life of every gathering he entered, and was always in demand as an after dinner orator. Stories of the jokes he played on other people are without end, and he enjoyed telling them; but I never knew him to tell one at his own expense, although they were numerous enough.

I remember an instance which took place at Springfield soon after our return from Europe. We persuaded a young musician of our troupe, Charlie Gill, who was never so happy as when playing a practical joke, to try to catch Mr. Barnum. So one night he raised the skin at the base of his palm with a needle, and inserted a sprig almost twelve inches long from a corn broom, so that only about a quarter of an inch was visible under the skin and the rest was hidden under his coat sleeve. As soon as Mr. Barnum entered the room, Charlie called out to our manager, "Oh, Mr. Wells, I've got a sliver in my hand, and I can't get it out! Have you got a pair of tweezers? It hurts like the mischief!"

Everybody knew that Mr. Barnum always carried a pair of tweezers; so Mr. Wells made only a pretense of searching his pockets.

"No Charlie," he said, "I haven't. Let me see your hand. Why, that looks pretty bad. You'd better go and see the doctor. You—"

"What's the matter there, Gill?" interrupted Mr. Barnum. "A splinter in your hand? Pooh! I'll fix that in a minute." He pulled out his tweezers and gently grasped the end of the sprig with them. Then carefully, so as not to hurt Charlie, he began to draw it out. You can imagine the laugh that burst out as the twelve inches of corn sprig emerged from under Charlie Gill's sleeve.

There are probably few persons alive to-day who have had as varied experience as I in the matter of vehicles for travel. I began my career long before the era of electricity, and some little time before steam cars had become a universal medium. Stages were still in use in the country districts in Massachusetts until after I first left home. The trains on which I went West with Colonel Wood were crude and uncomfortable, and the steamboats on which we traveled up and down the Mississippi were certainly picturesque and not lacking in excitement, if they offered nothing else.

Our trip across the continent in the early days of the Union Pacific was one that can never be duplicated. No Pullman cars, none of the conveniences which make traveling a pleasure nowadays, were then in vogue. The passage of time lends a sort of romance to those old fashioned modes of travel, but I can assure you there was nothing romantic in the actual experience. Our itinerary involved on the average one hundred and ten miles of traveling and two entertainments daily. The fact that we completed this tour without physical breakdown should be sufficient answer to the question as to whether we had mature bodies, whatever may be thought of our brains. . . .

Notes

NOTES TO THE INTRODUCTION

1. These later figures are given in an anonymous pamphlet written shortly after the wedding, *Sketch of the Life, Personal Appearance, Character and Manners of Charles S. Stratton, the Man in Miniature, Known as General Tom Thumb, and His Wife, Lavinia Warren Stratton* . . . (New York, 1863), p. 9. In its obituary of Lavinia published on 26 November 1919, the *New York Times* was still quoting them, although, as is evident from photographs of Lavinia in later life, she certainly must then have weighed more. In the obituary of Tom Thumb appearing in the *New York Daily Tribune* of 16 July 1883, it is stated that she then weighed around fifty pounds and stood around forty inches tall. Reliable measurements of dwarfs and giants, for obvious reasons, are often difficult to come by.

2. Readers too young to have had this privilege may nonetheless remember the craze for "Tom Thumb Weddings," got up by doting mothers across America to display their infants, which were popular until the time of the Second World War. The editor himself, at the tender age of three or four, played a leading role in one of these festivities, but was abandoned by his "Lavinia" immediately after the ceremony.

3. See Alice Curtis Desmond, "General Tom Thumb's Widow: The Autobiography of the Countess M. Lavinia Magri," in the New-York Historical Society *Quarterly*, XXXVIII (1954), 311–12.

4. Letter to Mrs. M. A. Powers, in the Barnum Museum, Bridgeport.

5. See Benjamin J. Bump, *The Story That Never Grows Old* (n.p., [1953]), unpaginated pamphlet.

6. Letter of 11 November 1878, in the Historical Collections, Bridgeport Public Library.

7. Bump, *The Story That Never Grows Old.*

8. See, e.g., Mertie E. Romaine, *General Tom Thumb and His Lady* (Taunton, Mass., 1976), p. 66.

9. Program in the Barnum Museum, Bridgeport.

10. A copy of the play is in the Barnum Museum.

11. Letter in the Barnum Museum.

12. On Lavinia's death and funeral, see the 26 and 30 November 1919 issues of this paper.

13. Undated clipping from the *New York Tribune* in the Westervelt Scrapbooks, "Barnum's Enterprises," VII, at the New-York Historical Society. For a full account of the auctions of Tom Thumb's and Lavinia's effects, and the whereabouts of many of these items today, see Romaine, pp. 71–82. The Barnum Museum in Bridgeport, it should be noted, recently acquired the Tom Thumb collection formerly at Sutro's Museum, Seal Rocks, San Francisco.

NOTES TO *The Autobiography of Mrs. Tom Thumb*

1. The anonymous visitor's logic was not all that uncommon, as is attested by a letter in the New-York Historical Society. Attending a reception at the White House to honor Lavinia and Tom Thumb shortly after their wedding in 1863, Mrs. G. V. Fox, who was evidently as amused as the President and Mrs. Lincoln were by their distinguished guests, could not help remarking that "I felt that their minds must be as limited as their bodies." Lavinia herself, as her manuscript reveals at several places, was sensitive on this score.

2. According to Lavinia's nephew Benjamin J. Bump, Lavinia's young pupils pulled her to school on their sleds and in bad weather carried her into the schoolhouse to keep her feet dry—*The Story That Never Grows Old.*

3. There was apparently some confusion in Lavinia's mind as to the precise identity of this cousin, whom she later terms both "Mr." and "Colonel" Wood. In her first draft she writes that "one day my mother was surprised by a visit from a distant relative, Mr. John Wood, brother to Col. Wood, the well-known museum manager and general amusement caterer of the West." Mr. John Wood, she continues, "furnished all of the living curiosities, paying his brother a certain share of the receipts for the privilege; the Colonel furnished the board and accommodations."

4. The last resident minstrel troupe in New York City, the San Francisco Minstrels performed there from 1865 until the winter of 1883–84 and were famous for their farcical skits featuring Billy Birch and Charley Backus. For a description of this company, see Robert C. Toll, *Blacking Up: The*

Minstrel Show in Nineteenth-Century America (New York: Oxford University Press, 1974), pp. 149–52. Both William H. Bernard and David Wambold were also minstrels, the former a noted interlocutor and the latter a ballad singer.

5. In the first draft Lavinia writes that some of the men on the boat declared they saw several of the attackers "drop."

6. The American Museum, which Barnum first became proprietor of in 1841 (from 1855 to 1860 it was in other hands), was one of New York's most famous sights. Thousands of curiosities, freaks and wild animals were displayed within its walls, while a large "lecture room"—in reality a well equipped theatre—exhibited edifying dramas such as *The Drunkard*. The building was destroyed by fire in July 1865. Four months later Barnum opened a New American Museum, which stood until it too was consumed by flames in March 1868. For descriptions of these buildings and their various attractions, see, in addition to Barnum's own autobiography, William W. Appleton, "The Marvellous Museum of P. T. Barnum," published in *Le Merveilleux et les arts du spectacle* (Actes du IIIe Congrès International d'Histoire du Théatre, 1963), pp. 57–62.

7. Lavinia's parents were not so far off the mark in their assessment of the character of Barnum, who proudly styled himself "Prince of Humbugs" and eloquently defended his practice of the art of humbug—which he defined not as deceptive or dishonest advertising, but as flashy publicity used to sell a reputable item or person—in his book *The Humbugs of the World* (New York, 1866). At the time Lavinia made his acquaintance some of his own more notable achievements in this line already included the decrepit, hymn-singing Negress known as Joice Heth, whom Barnum had billed as 161 years old and brazenly exhibited as the nurse of George Washington; the notorious "Fejee Mermaid," depicted in Barnum's publicity material as the beautiful bare-breasted creature of mythology, but in reality the body of a fish sewn to the hideous dessicated head and torso of a monkey; and, as Lavinia indicates, the phenomenally successful "General" Tom Thumb. Although certainly one of Barnum's more legitimate "curiosities," Tom Thumb was also "barnumized" at the outset of his career and was advertised, when he was slightly under five years old, as "a dwarf of eleven years of age, just arrived from England," so that people, as Barnum informs us in the first edition of his autobiography, would be assured "he was *really a dwarf*." As to the claim that the prodigy had arrived from England, when in fact he hailed from no more distant a locale than Bridgeport, Connecticut, the showman complacently adds that "if the announcement that he was *a foreigner* answered my purpose, the people had only themselves to blame if they did not get their money's worth when they visited the exhibition. I had observed . . . the American fancy for European exotics; and if the deception, practised for a season in my dwarf experiment, has done any thing towards checking our disgraceful preference for foreigners, I may readily be pardoned for the offence I here acknowledge"—*The Life of P. T. Barnum, Written by Himself* (New York, 1855), pp. 243–44. Mr. Neil Harris, in his excellent book *Humbug: The Art of P. T. Barnum* (Boston: Little, Brown,

1973), has focused on Barnum's career as a publicist and provides many telling descriptions and evaluations of his *modi operandi*.

8. Tom Thumb was twenty-four years old at the time of his first meeting with Lavinia. He had already acquired a considerable fortune through his association and tours with Barnum and was then living at his ease in his native Bridgeport, where Barnum himself had resided, in a series of mansions that would eventually number four, since 1848. For several years following his initial engagement with Barnum he was described in various publicity brochures and descriptive sketches of his life as standing 28 inches tall and weighing a little over 15 pounds (Barnum himself writes in his autobiography that Tom Thumb was "not two feet high" and weighed less than 16 pounds when he first saw him in November 1842). The General later sprouted in both height and girth, however, became a portly looking gentleman with a moustache and goatee, and at the time of his death in 1883 stood 40 inches tall and weighed 75 pounds.

9. As not infrequently happens when Lavinia is quoting from her sources, she has made a few changes and deletions in the original, including two references to her as a "dwarf." The original of the passage she quotes begins as follows: "In 1862 I heard of an extraordinary dwarf girl, named Lavinia Warren"—*Struggles and Triumphs: or, Forty Years' Recollections of P. T. Barnum, Written by Himself* (Buffalo, 1872), p. 582.

10. *Sketch of the Life, Personal Appearance, Character and Manners of Charles S. Stratton, the Man in Miniature, Known as General Tom Thumb, and His Wife, Lavinia Warren Stratton*, pp. 10–11.

11. This, too, a printed clipping pasted into the manuscript, is from the same pamphlet (p. 12) mentioned in the preceding note, as is Lavinia's letter to Barnum. Quite obviously, Lavinia's supposed annoyance at Barnum's not keeping his promise to first exhibit her before the "Courts of Europe" (where Tom Thumb had previously triumphed) was public knowledge, no doubt brought to light by the wily showman himself. In fact, it seems likely that the humbuggery so feared by Lavinia's parents a few months earlier was already in full swing, with Barnum characteristically manipulating the press and artfully enhancing the value of his latest acquisition preparatory to displaying her before the general public. The same strategy of limiting public exhibitions while holding private receptions for the "elite" had proved eminently successful when Barnum took Tom Thumb to England in 1844—and was now improved upon by the threat of a further postponement occasioned by a foreign tour.

That Lavinia herself, despite her reticence on the subject, was not totally averse to such publicity practices is attested by a widely circulated photograph, made after her marriage to Tom Thumb, in which she and the General pose side by side and Lavinia holds an infant in her lap. The obvious inference is that the baby is theirs; and on a medal that Barnum commissioned to publicize his museum around this time, the same scene of domestic bliss is repeated with the added information that the child is their "daughter, born Decr. 5, 1863." Both the photograph (of which there were at least two variations, one with Lavinia and the baby alone) and the medal have

183

confused some later writers, and the obituary of Tom Thumb in the *New York Times* for 16 July 1883 also mentions a child "born in Brooklyn fourteen years ago, who only lived two years." It seems certain Lavinia and Tom Thumb never had any children, however, and Lavinia's nephew Benjamin J. Bump later reported that the photograph was a hoax perpetrated by Barnum, who sold it for twenty-five cents a copy—see *The Story That Never Grows Old* and the letter of Edna L. Bump, wife of Benjamin, to the editor of the *New York Times*, 21 April 1946. In Europe, too, from occasional references in journals to Mr. and Mrs. Tom Thumb and "baby," it appears some people mistook Lavinia's sister Minnie for a child.

12. Mrs. James Gordon Bennett, wife of the famous editor and publisher of the *New York Herald* and frequent antagonist of Barnum. She was a talented musician and spent much of her time abroad, partly, it is said, on account of the attacks made on her by her husband's enemies. The editor is totally unacquainted with her indiscretions in Italy.

13. In this passage, too, Lavinia has considerably altered and abridged Barnum's account, tactfully omitting, for example, all references to the rivalry between Tom Thumb and Commodore Nutt for her hand. According to Barnum, Lavinia herself inadvertently encouraged the hopes of the latter by giving him a ring, and on one occasion he and Tom Thumb got into a "friendly scuffle" in the dressing room of the Museum. The showman also describes in detail the actual scene of Tom Thumb's proposing to Lavinia—secretly observed, or so he writes, by a "couple of mischievous young ladies" who were then staying at his house in Bridgeport—and the "sound of something very much like the popping of several corks from as many beer bottles" that followed Lavinia's acceptance—see the 1872 edition of *Struggles and Triumphs*, pp. 585–601.

14. Commodore Nutt (1844–81), a native of Manchester, New Hampshire, had been employed at the Museum for a year prior to Lavinia's arrival. He shortly got over his disappointment at Lavinia's engagement to Tom Thumb, agreed to serve as best man at their wedding, and afterward accompanied them on their tours, although he later went into the variety business on his own. His sobriquet the "$30,000 Nutt" derived from the terms of his initial three-year contract with Barnum, who additionally publicized him by ordering for his use a miniature carriage in the shape of an English walnut, now preserved in the Barnum Museum at Bridgeport. Although a number of writers have claimed he later suffered the additional humiliation of being rejected by Lavinia's sister Minnie on account of his "fast" living and remained a bachelor to the end, his obituary in the *New York Times* (26 May 1881) reports that two years previous to his death he married a Miss Lilian [*sic*] Elston, only a little below average height, who was seen sobbing over his coffin, calling him her "dear little boy." At the time of his initial engagement with Barnum he measured 30 inches, but by the time of his death had attained the height of 43 inches and become rather stout.

15. Although they are included in the first draft of the manuscript, here Lavinia decided to cross out Barnum's additional remarks on the wedding preparations, including a scandalous episode involving Bishop

Potter of New York, who originally agreed to perform the ceremony but then, under pressure from the more squeamish among his clergy, "rescinded his engagement." As is indicated in the passage quoted by Lavinia, Barnum paid for the wedding.

16. The two letters quoted by Lavinia were both originally published in Barnum's own autobiography.

17. The story of the blackmailing female was also originally published in Barnum's autobiography.

18. This tale of how Tom Thumb received his title, which Lavinia repeats later in her narrative, is not altogether accurate, for Barnum himself advertised his prodigy as "General Tom Thumb" from the very start of his career. It is conceivable, however, that the conversation related by Tom Thumb did indeed take place, with the Queen giving official sanction to Tom Thumb's use of the title. A similar story relates to the nineteenth-century English circus proprietor "Lord" George Sanger, who assumed his title out of pique with the rival showman "Buffalo Bill," whom English journalists customarily referred to as the "Honourable William Cody." Some time later, while parading his circus before the Queen in the courtyard of Windsor Castle, he was introduced to his sovereign as "Mr. Sanger." The Queen, who was obviously acquainted with his reputation, ironically remarked, "*Lord* George Sanger, I believe?" "Yes," stammered the showman, "if Your Majesty pleases!"

19. In the first draft of this passage Lavinia writes of her and Tom Thumb accepting invitations to the residences of "many of the élite of the city—General Frémont and wife, Mr. W. H. Vanderbilt, Mr. August Belmont, Mr. Brooks, etc. etc."

20. As this and several other incidents in Lavinia's narrative reveal, the touring troupe's exchequer was frequently jeopardized by the absence of modern banking practices. The sums of money and the value of the jewelry they carried with them were known to be considerable, and Bleeker and his charges had to keep a wary eye out for potential trouble.

21. Their "prices," as Lavinia writes in the first draft, were "twenty-five cents admission for adults and fifteen cents for children—no extra price for reserved seats."

22. The Prince refers to the first of three appearances Tom Thumb and Barnum made at Buckingham Palace during their initial trip to London in 1844. In his autobiography Barnum provides an amusing description of both his and Tom Thumb's conduct on this occasion, including Tom Thumb's encounter with the Queen's pet dog, mentioned later in Lavinia's narrative.

23. Prince Napoléon Eugène Louis Bonaparte (1856–79), who lived in England following the fall of the Second Empire in 1870, volunteered for the British expedition to Zululand and was killed there while out on a reconnaissance mission.

24. Jenny Lind (1820–87), later Mrs. Otto Goldschmidt, another of Barnum's highly profitable speculations, had given a total of ninety-five concerts in America under the showman's management from 11 September 1850 to 9 June 1851. Owing to the influence of some meddling "advisers" (or

so Barnum claims), she then broke with Barnum and continued on her own, although the two remained on friendly terms. Since 1856 she had made her home in England.

25. These are among the highest prices paid for tickets sold by auction to Jenny Lind's American concerts, as reported by Barnum in his autobiography. Genin, a hatter who occupied premises next to Barnum's museum, successfully bid for the first ticket to her inaugural concert at Castle Garden. The free publicity he received as a result of this shrewd investment, Barnum writes, "laid the foundation of his fortune."

26. The same Brettell was a friend of Barnum and previously had printed several pamphlets on Tom Thumb.

27. It seems obvious Lavinia had some difficulty separating the present tour of Britain from the one she and the same company made in 1871–72 toward the end of their three-year tour around the world. The figure of 208 cities and towns visited, for example, is the same as she reports for the later tour—to which it more properly applies, since Bleeker, whose published account of the world tour she relied on, himself gives this figure.

28. As was customary whenever they were on their tours, the company traveled to and from the exhibition hall in a miniature carriage drawn by ponies.

29. Phoenix Park, the site of Dublin's famous zoo, where Irish terrorists murdered the chief secretary and permanent undersecretary in 1882.

30. Since the original draft of the beginning of this chapter was also discarded, Lavinia's summary of its contents has been lost.

31. From this point in the manuscript until the commencement of chapter 20, Lavinia relies heavily on Bleeker's book, *Gen. Tom Thumb's Three Years' Tour around the World*.

32. Rodnia or Rodney Nutt Jr. was the brother of Commodore Nutt and had previously served as coachman to his brother during the latter's drives about New York in his walnut-shell carriage. As is obvious from his employment, he too was a dwarf.

33. Edward Zane Carroll Judson (1823–86), known to his readers as "Ned Buntline," was the prolific writer of dime novels and popularizer of the Buffalo Bill legend. He had previously served time in prison for inciting the mob during the Astor Place Riot in New York City and had been dishonorably discharged from the Union army in 1864.

34. According to Bleeker's account (p. 28), this arrangement led to some disruption in the parade's progress: "When the head of the fourth division, comprising several thousand schoolchildren, arrived at the hotel, the youngsters espied our 'little people'; the foremost raised the cry, 'Tom Thumb! Tom Thumb! Minnie Warren! Minnie Warren!' The shout was taken up by those behind, until it was echoed along the whole line. In their eagerness to press forward, they broke loose from all restraint; the teachers lost all control; the marshall's aids galloped hither and thither, frantically endeavoring to restore order, and casting angry glances at the unintentional authors of the commotion. I screened our little party from view, and finally order was again supreme."

35. It was Bleeker (p. 32), in fact, who refused to permit the Indians to enter the hall and informed Joseph that he alone was welcome.

36. "Them 'ar dwarfs make more excitement in the streets than an airthquake" (Bleeker, p. 37).

37. Bleeker's own account (p. 40) of this incident is rather unflattering to the General and Commodore, who were so frightened when the horses ran off that they "covered their ears, ran into the inn and closed the door to shut out the clattering sound."

38. The reference to Callahan's Ranch would seem to be out of place at this point, since both Bleeker and Lavinia, later in her narrative, mention stopping there after they had descended Scott's Mountain.

39. "Joss": the pidgin English word for Chinese gods in general.

40. Another anecdote, reported by Barnum in his autobiography and slightly altered by Lavinia in the retelling, concerning Tom Thumb's first meeting with the Prince of Wales in 1844.

41. As Lavinia writes, Tom Thumb was indeed trained by Barnum and the tutors he employed to "speak and act like a man." This passage is especially revealing for being the only expression of disapproval of Barnum and his promotional methods which the editor has discovered in any of Lavinia's writings.

42. It would appear Lavinia is here writing not about jugglers but street magicians, although the latter ("prestidigitateurs") have not always been considered so far removed from the former. Signor Antonio Blitz, Alexander Herrmann and his brother Carl, and Harry Kellar were all famous magicians who performed in America during the second half of the nineteenth century.

Bleeker himself (p. 60) was scandalized by the "vein of lewdness" he observed in the performances of Japanese "jugglers" and cautioned several female passengers against witnessing them. However, "female curiosity was too strong," as he writes, and after some half dozen ladies and their gallants had stopped to watch one of these exhibitions, he shortly saw the ladies "making a precipitate retreat, with heightened color, some covering their faces with their handkerchiefs, and the gentlemen following with confused countenances." Apparently Lavinia herself was not too upset by what she saw.

On another occasion, Bleeker informs us (pp. 60–62), the General expressed his curiosity about the Japanese bath houses, where he had heard men and women bathed in common and in full view of passersby on the street. The manager obligingly took him by the hand and led him to one such establishment, but as the General was too short to see the bathers from outside, he insisted on going inside. The naked men, women, and children, however, were themselves not entirely devoid of curiosity, and upon seeing Tom Thumb scrambled out of the water and crowded around him! On the way back to the hotel the General walked on for some time in silence, then remarked to his guide, "Mr. Bleeker, if we tell this to the folks at home they will not believe us; but it is *so!* Men and women bathing together with not a rag upon them, and they don't mind it a bit! Write and let P. T. (Barnum) know what we have seen. If he had that place, just as it is—men, women, and children, all—in the United States, it would be the biggest show he ever had."

43. Although the manuscript itself is inconclusive on the matter, the following story of the centipede, added during Lavinia's revision and written on a separate leaf, would see to come at this point. In her 16 December 1906 article in the *New York Tribune* (see the Appendix) she retells it and specifically assigns it to Nagasaki.

44. As is obvious from a crossed-out sentence in her previous note, Lavinia is here thinking of the continuous vaudeville performances begun by the managers B. F. Keith and E. F. Albee at their Boston theatre, the Bijou, in 1885 and the claim that they invented them.

45. The reference to "bald-headed men" is explained in Bleeker (p. 67), who remarks on the effeminacy, both on and off the stage, of these female impersonators, who allow their hair to grow long "that it may be dressed like a female's, and their finger-nails to be such a length that they require silver shields to protect them." Bleeker's own account of the Chinese theatre is much fuller than Lavinia's and contains an interesting description of its peculiar stage conventions.

46. "Captain" Djordji Costentenus, who in 1876 became one of Barnum's curiosities, was completely tattooed from his scalp to the soles of his feet. According to one account, he had received this forcible decoration while a prisoner in "Chinese Tartary, as punishment for engaging in rebellion against the King"—a claim that was naturally greeted with suspicion by some spectators. For another version of how he came to be tattooed (persecuted by Turks for his Christian faith), by one who knew him, see Robert Edmund Sherwood, *Here We Are Again: Recollections of an Old Circus Clown* (Indianapolis: Bobbs-Merrill, 1926), pp. 148–52.

47. So much so, writes Bleeker (p. 97), "that traffic at such hours was completely stopped, and the mayor was several times called upon to forbid 'General Tom Thumb's' carriage passing through Bourke-street." The mayor refused to accede to these demands, however, and defended Tom Thumb's right to use his carriage in traveling to and from his legitimate place of business. The solution to the problem, he concluded, would be to restrain public curiosity, although "he feared that would be a hopeless task, for upon several occasions when upon the street while the General was passing, he had his own curiosity so excited that he had forgotten his dignity as mayor, and ran pell-mell after him."

48. Robert Heller (1833–78) was another famous magician of the day who performed in America. He was also a fine pianist who often incorporated musical numbers into his stage entertainments.

49. Apparently the musicians who preceded the Tom Thumb Company were not so flattered, for in her first draft Lavinia writes that "the audience at the Theatre Royal became impatient, and calls for 'Gen. Tom Thumb' frequently drowned the sweet notes of the artistes, to their discomfort."

50. The laughing jackass is a curious species of bird. In America it

frequently makes its abode on university campuses, especially in the vicinity of faculty offices.

51. On the reliability of this figure, see note 27 above.

52. Bleeker's own narrative concludes at this point.

53. "Major" Edward Newell, to whom Minnie was married in July 1877, was also in show business and for a time traveled with the General Tom Thumb Company. In addition to singing, dancing, and giving impersonations, he was an expert roller skater and was sometimes billed as the "Skatorial Phenomenon." Although Lavinia herself is reticent on the subject, Minnie died in childbirth on 23 July 1878, and the baby itself, which weighed nearly six pounds, died a few hours later. It was assumed by everyone that the baby, like its parents, would be a dwarf. Minnie herself, at her greatest height, measured only 32 inches.

54. Since 1871 Barnum had devoted much of his time to circus management and in 1881, in partnership with James A. Bailey and James L. Hutchinson, formed the great concern that eventually became known as "Barnum & Bailey." After the death of Bailey in 1906, the Ringling Brothers acquired control of the "Greatest Show on Earth" and in 1919 merged it with their own circus.

55. Tom Thumb died at Middleboro on 15 July 1883. Lavinia was reported in the newspapers as being then in Cincinnati.

56. Lavinia herself was eventually interred at Mountain Grove Cemetery, next to her first husband. The insignia of the Knights Templar is incised on Tom Thumb's small tombstone, and a few years ago the emblem of the Daughters of the American Revolution was affixed to Lavinia's. The family monument itself, a few feet beyond their graves, is crowned by a life-size statue of Tom Thumb, representing him at the height of his fame while under Barnum's management. The shaft supporting the statue was originally much taller, but had to be replaced, by a shorter one, in the present century. Barnum's own massive monument is across and a few feet up the road from Tom Thumb's. The cemetery is today one of the most picturesque areas of Bridgeport—the city itself having deteriorated so greatly since Barnum and Tom Thumb made their homes there—and is well worth a visit. For additional information on Barnum's association with Bridgeport and his continuing "presence" there, see, besides his own autobiography, A. H. Saxon, "Barnum à Bridgeport," *Le Cirque dans l'Univers*, no. 83 (4e trimestre 1971), pp. 25–30.

57. At this point in the manuscript the leaves in the first-draft state cease, and from this fact and the "contents" at the head of the chapter, it seems Lavinia orginally ended her narrative here. The final six leaves of the manuscript were all written during her later revision.

58. Both Count Primo and Baron Ernesto Magri, who bore papal titles, were members of the new touring company formed after Lavinia decided to renew her travels. They had been born at Bologna into a family of thirteen children, three of whom were dwarfs (the third, a daughter named Amalia, died at the age of twenty-four), and began exhibiting themselves in 1865. The Count himself stood 37 inches tall and weighed 55 pounds at the

time of his death, aged seventy-one, in 1920; his brother was around an inch and a half taller than he and predeceased him in Boston. Sarah Adams and her sister Lucy, natives of Martha's Vineyard, were also dwarfs and at one time traveled with the Tom Thumb Company.

59. Robert-Houdin (1805–71) was the greatest French magician of the nineteenth century. On Blitz and Herrmann, see note 42 above.

Notes to the Appendix

1. In her article "General Tom Thumb's Widow: The Autobiography of the Countess M. Lavinia Magri," Mrs. Desmond reports (p. 311) that in the fall of 1906 the condensed version appeared "in three issues of the *Theater Magazine*, and in the *New York Tribune Sunday Section*." It is obvious she was confused, for a thorough check of all issues of the *Theatre Magazine*—originally titled *The Theatre: Illustrated Monthly Magazine of Dramatic and Musical Art*—from its first issue in 1900 through its thirty-first volume in 1920 revealed no excerpts from Lavinia's autobiography. Very likely Mrs. Desmond came across clippings, perhaps misidentified, in the collections where she did her research.

2. This is a variation of a story Barnum tells, at considerably greater length, in the thirty-seventh chapter of his autobiography.

Selected Bibliography

BARNUM, PHINEAS TAYLOR. *The Life of P. T. Barnum, Written by Himself*. New York: Redfield, 1855. The first edition of the famous autobiography, completed by Barnum in 1854, which caused a furor on both sides of the Atlantic. Some of its more blatant episodes were considerably muted in subsequent editions.

————. *Struggles and Triumphs: or, Forty Years' Recollections of P. T. Barnum, Written by Himself*. Buffalo: Warren, Johnson & Co., 1872. The edition Lavinia herself apparently possessed and quotes from in her autobiography.

————. *Struggles and Triumphs: or, The Life of P. T. Barnum, Written by Himself*. Edited and introduced by George S. Bryan. 2 vols. New York & London: Alfred A. Knopf, 1927. The best scholarly edition, based on the 1855, 1869, and 1889 editions of Barnum's autobiography, with notes, several appendices, bibliography, many interesting illustrations, and a fine introduction by the editor.

BLEEKER, SYLVESTER. *Gen. Tom Thumb's Three Years' Tour around the World, Accompanied by His Wife—Lavinia Warren Stratton, Commodore Nutt, Miss Minnie Warren, and Party*. New York: S. Booth, [1872].

191

BUMP, BENJAMIN J. *The Story That Never Grows Old.* No place: no publisher, [1953]. An unpaginated pamphlet consisting of only eight pages of text, but which nonetheless contains several interesting anecdotes of Lavinia and her husbands, by Lavinia's nephew, who eventually became principal of the high school at Harwich, Mass.

DESMOND, ALICE CURTIS. *Barnum Presents: General Tom Thumb.* New York: Macmillan, 1954. Although written for children and somewhat fictionalized, Mrs. Desmond's book possesses considerable merit, since she herself, as she tells us in the "Author's Afterword," lived in Bridgeport until the time of her marriage, knew or was personally related to many persons who were associated with Tom Thumb and Barnum, and made extensive use of research materials in Bridgeport, New York, and elsewhere.

————. "General Tom Thumb's Widow: The Autobiography of the Countess M. Lavinia Magri." The New-York Historical Society *Quarterly,* XXXVIII (1954), 310–24.

ROMAINE, MERTIE E. *General Tom Thumb and His Lady.* Taunton, Mass.: William S. Sullwold, [1976]. By one who as a young girl knew Mrs. Tom Thumb and was formerly chief librarian at the Middleborough Public Library.

SAXON, A. H. "Barnum à Bridgeport." *Le Cirque dans l'Univers,* no. 83 (4e trimestre 1971), pp. 25–30. Describes the several collections of Tom Thumb and Barnum memorabilia in Bridgeport today and other sights associated with the city's two most famous residents.

Sketch of the Life, Personal Appearance, Character and Manners of Charles S. Stratton, the Man in Miniature, Known as General Tom Thumb, and His Wife, Lavinia Warren Stratton, Including the History of Their Courtship and Marriage. . . . Also, Songs Given at Their Public Levees. New York: Wynkoop, Hallenbeck & Thomas, 1863. This pamphlet went through several editions.

Sketch of the Life, Personal Appearance, Character and Manners of Charles S. Stratton, the Man In Miniature, Known as General Tom Thumb, Fifteen Years Old, Twenty-Eight Inches High, and Weighing Only Fifteen Pounds. With Some Account of Remarkable Dwarfs, Giants, and Other Human Phenomena, of Ancient and Modern Times. Also, General Tom Thumb's Songs. New York: Van Norden & Amerman, 1847. There were many editions of this pamphlet published in America and abroad.

Index of Persons

Adams, Lucy, 170–71, 190 n. 58
Adams, Sarah, 170, 190 n. 58
Albee, E. F., 188 n. 44
Alexandra (Princess of Wales, later
  Queen of England), 76
Andrew ("Andrews"), John
  Albion (Governor of
  Massachusetts), 52
Argyle, Duchess of, 79
Babot (ship captain), 129
Backus, Charley, 181 n. 4
Bailey, James A., 189 n. 54
Barnum, P. T., 14–15, 32, 37,
  48–60 passim, 64–65, 69, 178–
  79, 185 n. 22; always an
  entertainer, 178; American
  Museum of, 182 n. 6;
  Bridgeport residences of, 183 n.
  8; butt of practical joke, 178–79;
  circus of, 189 n. 54; discovers
  and engages Lavinia, 10, 48–50,
  183 n. 9; discovers and tutors
  Tom Thumb, 10, 115–16, 187
  n. 41, 189 n. 54; forms General
  Tom Thumb Company, 57, 65;
  gives up interest in company,
  14, 166–67; humbuggery of, 32,
  49, 178, 182–83 n. 7, 183–84 n.
  11; laughs at blackmail attempt,
  60; monument of, 189 n. 56;
  pays for Lavinia's wedding, 57,
  185 n. 15; proposes world tour,
  97–98; tries to defer wedding,
  57–58; urges Lavinia to
  continue in show business, 170,
  173
Beatrice, Princess, 77–78
Benares, King of, 155, 176
Bennett, Mrs. James Gordon, 54,
  184 n. 12
Bernard, William H., 182 n. 4
Birch, Billy, 42, 181 n. 4
Birch, Mrs. Billy, 42
Bleeker, Sylvester, 11, 14, 16–17,
  31–32, 65–170 passim, 177, 185
  n. 20, 187 nn. 35 and 42; laughs
  at Lavinia's solicitude, 115;
  manhandles Chinese actors, 125;
  prevents panic in theatre, 68–69
Bleeker, Mrs. Sylvester, 95–169
  passim; death of, 169
Blitz, Antonio, 118, 173, 187 n. 42

195

Bonaparte, Napoléon Eugène Louis (Prince Imperial), 77, 185 n. 23
Booth, John Wilkes, 72–73
Brady, Mathew B., 15
Brettell, T. (printer), 83–84, 186 n. 26
Brettell, Mrs. T., 83–85
Bryant, Dan, 65
Bump, Benjamin (Lavinia's brother), 18, 63
Bump, Benjamin J. (Lavinia's nephew), 181 n. 2, 184 n. 11
Bump, Edna L. (wife of Benjamin J.), 184 n. 11
Bump, James S. (Lavinia's father), 9, 34
Bump, Huldah P. (Lavinia's mother), 9, 34
Bump, Huldah Pierce (Lavinia's sister). See Warren, Minnie
Bump, Mercy Lavinia Warren. See Warren, Lavinia
Burnside, General Ambrose Everett, 53
Cambridge, Duke of, 76
Churchill, Rhoda, 81
Cody, William F. ("Buffalo Bill"), 185 n. 18
Colfax, Schuyler, 108, 112
Cooper, G. (groom), 98
Costentenus, "Captain" Djordji, 127, 188 n. 46
Crocker (judge), 112
Crocker, Charles, 112
Crowell (ship captain), 126
Davis, Edmund, 98
Davis, Jefferson (and family), 176
Desmond, Alice Curtis, 12, 190 n. 1
Doane (ship captain), 113
Dodge, Ossian E., 78
Douglas, Stephen A., 44–45
Dunbar, Mr. (Lavinia's teacher), 36–37
Edinburgh, Duke of, 147–48

Edmunds, Lizzie (wife of Morris), 44
Edmunds, Morris, 44
Edward (Prince of Wales, later Edward VII), 76, 79, 85, 115
Elston, Lilian, 184 n. 14
Emma (Queen of Sandwich Islands), 90
Eugénie (Empress of the French), 77
Faiber, Ernestine de. See fig.
"Fejee Mermaid," 182 n. 7
Fitzgerald, Captain (Union officer), 73
Francis Joseph I (Emperor), 166
Franklin, Lady (widow of polar explorer), 90
Furber, W. G. (ship captain), 118
Genin, John N., 78, 186 n. 25
Gill, Charlie, 178–79
Goulding, Colonel (American consul), 126
Grant, Frederick Dent, 71
Grant, Ulysses S., 11, 44 (and family), 70–71
Hardy, Miss (giantess), 41
Helena, Princess, 78
Heller, Robert, 141, 188 n. 48
Herrmann, Alexander, 118, 173, 187 n. 42
Herrmann, Carl, 118, 173, 187 n. 42
Heth, Joice, 182 n. 7
Humbert (Prince, later King of Italy), 166
Hunter, General David, 69
Hutchinson, James L., 189 n. 54
Johore, Maharajah of, 129–31
Johore, Maharini of, 130–31
Judson, Edward Zane Carroll ("Ned Buntline"), 100, 186 n. 33
Keeler, C. E., 98
Keith, B. F., 188 n. 44
Kellar, Harry, 118, 187 n. 42
Kellogg, B. S., 98

196

Khedive of Egypt, 163
Kimball, Heber, 104
Lee, General Robert E., 176
Leopold, Prince, 78
Lincoln, President Abraham, 61–62
Lincoln, Mrs. Abraham, 61–62, 176 (and mother)
Lincoln, "Tad" (Thomas), 62
Lind, Jenny (Mrs. Otto Goldschmidt), 78, 185–86 n. 24
Logrenia, "Professor" (magician), 18
Louise, Princess, 78
McAllister, J. D. T., 104
McClellan, General George Brinton, 53
MacDonald, Sir Richard Graves, 126
McPherson, General James Birdseye, 53
Magri, Amalia, 189 n. 58
Magri, Baron Ernesto, 17–18, 170–72, 189–90 n. 58; family of, 172
Magri, Countess M. Lavinia. See Warren, Lavinia
Magri, Count Primo, 12, 17–19, 170–72, 189–90 n. 58; death of, 19; height and weight of, 190 n. 58
Margherita ("Marguerite") (Princess of Savoy, later Queen of Italy), 166
Mayo, Lord (Viceroy of India), 153
Monck ("Monk"), Lord and Lady, 67–68
Morgan, General John Hunt, 73, 176–77
Napoléon III (Emperor of the French), 77
Newell, "Major" Edward, 169–71, 189 n. 53
Newman, John (Cardinal), 76
Nobbs, F. G., 98

Norton, Miss (guest), 84–85
Nutt, "Commodore" George Washington Morrison, 11, 57, 65–169 passim, 177, 184 nn. 13 and 14; entertainments of, 123; "forages" for food, 71–72, 176; height of, 184 n. 14; leaves a sobbing widow, 184 n. 14
Nutt, Rodnia or Rodney Jr., 98, 186 n. 32
Parr, Thomas, 81
Potter, Bishop Horatio, 184–85 n. 15
Putnam, Rev. I. W., 34, 58
Richardson, G. H., 98
Robert-Houdin (Jean Eugène Robert), 173, 190 n. 59
Robinson, Sir Hercules, 138–39
Robinson, Leonard M., 12
Root, M. A., 78
Rosecrans ("Rosencrans"), General William Starke, 53
Ross, Colonel W. C., 78
Sanger, "Lord" George, 185 n. 18
Saxe-Weimar, Duke and Duchess of, 91
Scott, General Winfield, 53
Skottowe (ship captain), 140
Smith, Albert, 11
Smith, Dr. and Mrs. L. L., 141
Snow, Lorenzo, 105
"Springing Panther" (Indian), 105–106
Stanton, Edwin McMasters, 61–62
Stoddard ("Colonel Stodare" or John English, magician?), 116
Stratton, Charles Sherwood. See Tom Thumb
Stratton, Mrs. Charles Sherwood. See Warren, Lavinia
Sundahram (Indian landlord), 150
Taylor, Rev. (rector of Grace Church), 58–60
Tom Thumb, "General" (Charles Sherwood Stratton), 55–170 passim, 177–78, 183–84 n. 11,

197

185 n. 22; "barnumized," 182 n.
7; builds house after world tour,
171; careless with money and
jewels, 117, 167–68; death of,
17, 169, 189 n. 55; early bad
habits of, 116; embroiders, 77;
entertainments of, 10–12, 123;
excellent qualities of, 169;
funeral of, 170; grave and family
monument of, 170, 189 n. 56;
height and weight of, 183 n. 8;
"heroism" of, 187 n. 37; kisses
Blarney Stone, 91; never had
any childhood, 115–16, 169–70;
photographs of, 15, 57, 183–84
n. 11; receives title from Queen
Victoria, 62, 76, 185 n. 18;
rivalry of, with Commodore
Nutt, 184 n. 13; ties up traffic
with his carriage, 11, 75, 188 n.
47; visits Japanese bathhouse,
187–88 n. 42; woos and wins
Lavinia, 55–56
Tom Thumb, Mrs. "General." *See*
Warren, Lavinia
Topsey (Lavinia's dog), 172
Tucker (riverboat captain), 40
Victor Emmanuel II (King of
Italy), 166
Victoria (Queen of England), 11,
62, 76–79, 85, 185 n. 18
Vizianagram, Maharajah of, 150
Wales, Prince of. *See* Edward
Wales, Princess of. *See* Alexandra
Wambold, David, 182 n. 4
Ward, Lord (Earl of "Derby," i.e.
Dudley), 78
Warren, General Joseph, 33
Warren, Lavinia (née Mercy
Lavinia Warren Bump, later
Mrs. Charles S. Stratton or
"Mrs. Genl. Tom Thumb,"
then Countess M. Lavinia
Magri): ancestry of, 33–34;
avoids use of word "dwarf," 16,
183 n. 9; Barnum's "pet," 178;

birth of, 9, 34; "child" of, 183–
84 n. 11; death and funeral of,
19; determines to continue in
show business, 172–73;
disapproves of Barnum's training
of Tom Thumb, 115–16, 187 n.
41; distrusts diamond merchant,
89–90; embarks on career in
show business, 39–40;
entertainments of, 11–12, 17–
19, 123; escapes Ku Klux Klan,
95–97; frightened by centipede,
119; frightened by
somnambulist, 177; grave of,
189 n. 56; height and weight of,
9, 36, 180 n. 1; indignation of,
at Mormon polygamy, 102; joins
Barnum's circus for one season,
169; later reverses of, 16–17;
marries Count Primo Magri, 17,
170–71; marries Tom Thumb,
10, 58–59; meets Tom Thumb,
49; not "dead all over yet," 173;
patriotism of, 76–77, 171;
photographs of, 15, 57, 183–84
n. 11; physical perfection of,
50–51; possessions of, auctioned
off, 19, 181 n. 13; public
persona of, 16; quotes scripture,
35–36; reception of, at White
House, 61–62; reflects on crime
and punishment, 46–47; refuses
gift of slave, 176; "sleepwalks,"
152–53; teaching career of, 38,
181 n. 2; viewed as bad omen by
Chinese, 126; writes
autobiography, 12–14, 175
Warren, Minnie (Huldah Pierce
Bump), 11, 37–38, 65–169
passim, 177, 184 n. 11; birth of,
9, 34; death of, 168, 189 n. 53;
enters Barnum's employ, 10, 57;
flirts with Duke of Edinburgh,
148; height of, 189 n. 53
Watkins, Rev., 170
Wellington, Duke of, 62

Wells (manager), 179
Wells, George A., 56–57
West, Bishop, 101–102
Whitlock, C. E. H., 12
Willey, Rev. (Tom Thumb's pastor), 58

Wood, "Colonel" John (?), 39–49 passim, 176, 179, 181 n. 3
Woodruff, Wilford, 104
Yorke, Sir Elliot, 147
Young, Brigham, 103–104
Young, John, 103–104